80/20 YOUR LIFE!

HOW TO GET MORE DONE WITH LESS EFFORT AND CHANGE YOUR LIFE IN THE PROCESS!

DAMON ZAHARIADES

ARTOFPRODUCTIVITY.COM

CONTENTS

Are you constantly distracted? Does your mind wander after just a few minutes? Learn how to develop laser-sharp focus!

Small Habits Revolution

Got 5 minutes a day? Use this simple, effective plan for creating any new habit you desire!

To-Do List Formula

Finally! A step-by-step system for creating to-do lists that'll actually help you to get things done!

The 30-Day Productivity Plan

Need a daily action plan to boost your productivity? This 30-day guide is the solution to your time management woes!

The Time Chunking Method

It's one of the most popular time management strategies used today. Double your productivity with this easy 10-step system.

Digital Detox

Are you addicted to Facebook and Instagram? Are you obsessed with your phone? Use this simple, step-by-step plan to take a technology vacation!

For a complete list, please visit

http://artofproductivity.com/my-books/

YOUR FREE GIFT

~

As my way of saying thank you for purchasing *80/20 Your Life!*, I'd like to offer you my 40-page action guide titled *Catapult Your Productivity! The Top 10 Habits You Must Develop To Get More Things Done.*

It's in PDF format, so you can print it out easily and read it at your leisure. This guide will show you how to develop core habits that'll help you to get more done in less time.

You can get immediate access to *Catapult Your Productivity* by clicking the link below and joining my mailing list:

http://artofproductivity.com/free-gift/

WHAT IS THE 80/20 RULE AND HOW WILL IT IMPROVE YOUR LIFE?

~

T he 80/20 rule, also known as the Pareto principle, was the brainchild of Vilfredo Pareto, an Italian economist. In 1896, he noted that 80% of the property and wealth in Italy was owned by 20% of the population. No one is surprised by this notion today, but it was a heady proclamation at the time.

Pareto didn't stop with property and wealth distribution. He later showed the 80/20 rule could be applied to other phenomena. For example, he noted that 20% of the pea pods in his garden produced 80% of the peas. This discovery was later extrapolated by Pareto and others to demonstrate the veracity of the 80/20 rule in science, sports, economics, and software development.

Today, the 80/20 rule is typically discussed in the

context of business and workplace productivity. We're going to take a different approach. We're going to apply this simple, life-changing concept to every aspect of your daily experience. You'll find the 80/20 rule is a powerful tool that you can use to achieve maximum satisfaction from your career, home life, and relationships. It can have an enormous impact on your diet, physical fitness, finances, and education. It can propel your small business to remarkable success in a surprisingly short time frame.

In short, I'm going to show you how to use the 80/20 rule to optimize every area your life.

What the 80/20 Rule Isn't

This isn't about implementing a system. We're not trying to squeeze your life into a stodgy formula. Rather, this is about cultivating a forward-thinking mindset, one that recognizes the tremendous value in focusing on items that matter and ignoring the rest.

Nor is this about minimalism. While the Pareto principle can help you move *toward* minimalism (if that's your goal), its practical applications extend much further.

A common misconception of the 80/20 rule is that it encourages doing things in a hasty, careless manner. But that's untrue. We're not trying to cut corners. Instead, we're dedicating our focus and energy to tasks that produce the greatest impact with regards to our goals.

In other words, why spend our limited time on things that have a negligible effect on whatever we're trying to accomplish? If we can get 80% of the way there with only 20% of the effort, why not do so?

This idea will become crystal clear as we progress through *80/20 Your Life!*

The Name Of The Game Is Leverage

At its simplest, the Pareto principle is about leverage. This leverage allows you to do small things that can literally transform your life.

Think of the many ways we use leverage today. We use bottle openers to remove metal bottle caps. We use hammer claws to remove nails. We use car jacks to lift our vehicles when we need to change tires. We use scissors, which is a combination of two levers, to cut through paper, cardboard, and rope.

Other levers have little to do with physical force, but are just as useful. For example, a simple flick of a switch bathes an entire room in light. Depressing a trigger engages a drill, which can be used for a myriad of household projects.

I'm going to show you how to use the leverage promised by the 80/20 rule to dramatically improve every facet of your lifestyle.

80/20 Your Life! Is Open-Ended

Again, it's not my intent to give you a blueprint. I'm not interested in providing a plug-and-play formula. In my opinion, such an approach would do more harm than good. Any application of the Pareto principle should complement your circumstances.

Your circumstances are unique to *you*.

My goal in *80/20 Your Life!* is to inspire you to brainstorm - and experiment with - ways to apply the Pareto principle in your own daily experience. I'll give you a number of examples along the way, some of which come from my own life. You'll discover how I've used the 80/20 rule, and the leverage it offers, to make considerable changes in my lifestyle.

But these examples should serve only as a springboard for your own ideas. The 80/20 rule should reflect the context of your life and complement your personal goals.

It's my sincere hope that you'll become as enthusiastic as I am about the life-changing potential of the Pareto principle. I'm convinced you'll find that after you apply it to one area of your life and witness the results, you'll want to apply it everywhere!

MY 80/20 LIFESTYLE

(OR HOW THE PARETO PRINCIPLE WAS A GAME CHANGER FOR ME)

❧

I stumbled onto the 80/20 rule while attending college. It was a revelation to me. Today, decades later, it's still the measuring stick I use when deciding how and where to spend my time.

Having said that, it took me years to discover the true potential of the 80/20 rule. I had a limited perspective in college. I spent most of my time on school-related tasks, such as completing assignments and projects and studying for exams. That solitary focus constrained my understanding of the 80/20 rule. I applied the rule to all things related to my studies, but failed to intuit its wider applications.

It wasn't until much later that I began to comprehend the spectacular usefulness of the Pareto principle toward

other ends. Here's a glimpse at how my perception
expanded over the years.

In Corporate America

I learned quickly that not all meetings were worth attending. The majority were a waste of time (for me). So I
started skipping those, focusing on meetings where my
presence was actually necessary.

Numerous problems surfaced during the course of a
typical day. It was tempting to treat each of them with the
same level of attention. But I learned that some problems
were unimportant and best ignored for the sake of moving
forward.

Emails and instant messages were out of control at my
workplace. The volume was overwhelming as everyone
CC'd everyone else to "keep folks in the loop." I learned I
could ignore most emails and messages. I also discovered
that those relevant to my work rarely required a response
from me.

Running My Own Business

I started a small business in the early aughts. Time was
precious to me as I was still working 50 to 60 hours a week
at my job. So I needed a way to grow my business with a
minimal investment of time.

I used many of the lessons I learned in Corporate
America. For example, I avoided unnecessary meetings and

phone calls. I ignored nonessential emails. When I needed outside help, I avoided the typical back-and-forth that's par for the course for hiring folks.

I also found that 80% of my business's revenue came from 20% of its customers (the ratio was actually around 87/13). I had heard about this phenomenon, but running this business allowed me to witness it firsthand. It was a powerful lesson for me. It drove home the inarguable validity of the Pareto principle.

My Relationships

While attending college I read Dale Carnegie's classic book *How To Win Friends and Influence People*. I craved more connections and thought having a large number of friends was the solution.

Carnegie's advice worked better than I dreamed. Within a month, I was constantly surrounded by people who desired my attention. Unfortunately, it was a hollow success. The "friendships" I developed were shallow. Consequently, the time I spent nurturing them was less than rewarding.

That same year I began to cut back. Friendships that caused me stress were the first to go on the chopping block. Those with whom I shared little in common were next. I eventually reduced my circle of friends to a handful. The upside was that these were the friends I truly enjoyed and looked forward to seeing.

My Physical Health

My health suffered during my tenure in Corporate America. I ate everything in sight (most of it loaded with sugar) and got little exercise. Predictably, my weight increased and my physique ballooned.

When I finally became serious about getting into shape, I applied the 80/20 rule to my fitness strategy. Rather than eating like a rabbit, I simply cut out foods filled with processed sugar. That single tactic had an astounding effect on my weight and physique.

Rather than joining a gym and subjecting myself to intense daily workouts, I took short walks and did pushups. Again, the effects were immediately noticeable.

Focusing on the 20% of possible actions and ignoring the rest was a game changer when it came to my health.

My Writing

I've been applying the Pareto principle to my writing for more than 20 years.

When I'm in research mode, I resist the temptation to read everything written about the topic I'm investigating. Instead, I focus on studies that boast a large number of legitimate citations. Doing so helps me to focus on the *best* material.

When I create marketing campaigns to promote my books, I avoid social media, blog tours, book signings, guest blogging, and podcast interviews. I've learned these activities have a negligible effect on sales. Instead, I focus my time and attention on creating actionable content for my email newsletter and creating small ads on Amazon. These activities comprise the 20% of possible actions that produces 80% of my results.

When I'm writing a new book, I constantly remind myself that the first draft can include mistakes. Rather than self-editing to perfect the first draft, I set my internal editing gauge at 20%. If I misspell a word, I'll fix it. If I commit a terrible grammatical faux pas, I'll correct it. But otherwise, my goal is to get the first draft 80% of the way toward completion. The *real* editing comes later.

Letting Go Of My Obsessiveness

The 80/20 rule informs the majority of my decisions in every aspect of my life. It was an epiphany when I first discovered it, and my grasp of its potential has only grown over the years.

Allowing the Pareto principle to guide my decisions has forced me to abandon my obsessiveness over small tasks and details. That's a good thing. The small stuff rarely matters. Focusing on the big stuff, the 20%, saves valuable time, ramps up productivity, and moves the needle further when it comes to goal achievement.

The Pareto Principle Can Change Your Life

I'm 100% confident that the 80/20 rule can help you to design a more rewarding lifestyle. When you focus on the things that matter and ignore everything else, you'll make huge strides toward whatever goal you're trying to accomplish. Even better, you'll be able to do so with a minimum investment of time and energy.

In the following section, we'll take a look at the many practical reasons to adopt the Pareto principle in everything you do. Fair warning: I intend to convince you to *80/20 Your Life!*

10 COMPELLING REASONS TO 80/20 YOUR LIFE!

∾

The core idea behind the 80/20 rule is that you can get more done while taking less action. Once you recognize that a large proportion of your output results from a small proportion of inputs, you'll be able to truly leverage your time, focus, and effort.

This leverage will help you to transform your life. It'll help you to get more of what you really *want* out of your life by ignoring the unnecessary.

Below, I'll highlight ten practical benefits you'll enjoy when you adopt the 80/20 rule. Some may be more important to you than others. But applying this principle in everything you do will allow you to tap into all of them.

Let's get started.

1. Improved Time Management

Most people spend an inordinate amount of time on low-value tasks. This prevents them from advancing *important* projects. It's no surprise so many folks feel as if they're spinning their wheels while racing against time.

Many tasks can be outsourced. Some can be ignored entirely without consequence. By prioritizing high-value tasks and putting the rest on the back burner, you can regain control of your time. You'll be able to spend your time in areas where it'll have the greatest impact and give you the greatest sense of achievement.

2. Increased Efficiency And Productivity

Have you ever worked all day, yet felt as if you accomplished little? Perhaps you looked at your to-do list to confirm that you actually got stuff done. But you still feel as if you spent the day treading water.

That feeling stems from focusing your attention on nonessential activities. Perhaps you've completed everything on your to-do list, but none of the items you've crossed off have made a significant impact toward your goals.

This feeling evaporates when you "80/20" your life. Your efficiency and productivity go through the proverbial roof when you focus on the important and disregard the unimportant.

3. Faster Decision-Making

We face tough decisions every day. We possess limited resources (e.g. time, money, attention, etc.) and must spend them in a way that allows us to get the most out of them.

But making such decisions is often difficult. The most favorable options are unclear when we place equal importance on competing demands. And so we hesitate. We fear making the wrong choices and become paralyzed with inaction.

The Pareto principle offers a simple way out of this mental quagmire. It allows us to quickly identify demands that are inconsequential to our goals. That speeds up the decision-making process as irrelevant demands fade away.

4. Enhanced Focus

One of the greatest challenges we face today is an endless list of things that demand our attention. The more things we pay attention to, the more we dilute our attentional resources.

In the workplace, a continuous string of tasks, projects, and meetings demand our attention. At home, we're confronted by various chores, hobbies, and small emergencies. Most of us maintain too many relationships, and end up spending valuable time on those we don't enjoy.

The 80/20 rule helps us to optimize our focus, zeroing in on the things that truly matter to us. As a result, we feel more effective, more productive, and ultimately happier.

5. Greater Creativity

Stress is a common obstacle to creativity. That's certainly the case for me. When I'm worried about things, it's difficult for me to pursue and maintain divergent thinking. My attention becomes scattered and the creative part of my brain shuts down.

Fortunately, I've learned over the years that most of the things that trigger my unease are not worth my attention. This is consistent with the Pareto principle. Eighty percent of the items that cause me concern never come to pass. Therefore, they can be ignored without consequence.

When you 80/20 your life, you'll feel more creative. Your headspace won't be overwhelmed by the trivial minutiae that might otherwise cause you stress.

6. More Rewarding Relationships

You probably have friends with whom you don't truly enjoy spending time. Perhaps they're abrasive. Maybe they're shallow. They might be rude to others, which embarrasses you. Or they're surrounded by drama, which you find exhausting.

Whatever the case, these friends likely make up the 80% of your relationships that contribute little to your happiness.

When I focused on the few friends with whom I truly connected, I immediately felt happier. The emotional bonds were stronger. The sense of intimacy was deeper. Accordingly, those relationships felt more gratifying to me.

7. Better Leadership

It's tough being a leader. You're expected to always know what's best, make smart decisions, adeptly allocate resources, and communicate in a clear, inspiring manner.

That's a lot to ask. Whether you're a senior manager in Corporate America, the head of a local charity, or the voice of authority in your household, leadership is a tough gig.

The responsibility is easier to shoulder when you follow the 80/20 rule.

For example, making smart decisions requires information. But most of the information you can gather regarding any given topic is likely to prove immaterial. Some of it will do more harm than good, causing paralysis by analysis. By focusing on the 20% that matters, you can accelerate the decision-making process and feel comfortable owning your choices.

The Pareto principle has far-reaching implications with regard to leadership. We'll explore this in greater detail later.

8. Less Procrastination

You're more likely to procrastinate when you feel overwhelmed. If you've ever visited Facebook, browsed Instagram, or incessantly checked your email with a ton of work waiting in the wings, you know this from firsthand experience. The brain looks for distractions.

But the 80/20 rule states that most of the tasks demanding your attention are trivial. You can confidently disregard them.

Once you clear your plate of the noncritical tasks, you'll be more inclined to take action on the few important ones that remain.

9. Avoidance Of Information Overload

We touched on this above in the context of accelerating the decision-making process. But it's worth highlighting in its own regard.

Information overload occurs when the volume of information you possess obfuscates an issue and hampers your ability to learn or make decisions. It's akin to taking a sip of water from a firehose.

As we discussed above, 80% of the information you can gather about a topic is useless. It serves only to erode your focus and pointlessly complicate matters. You're better off ignoring it.

Whether you're about to make an important decision or learn a new skill, the 80/20 rule will help you to avoid becoming mired in over-analysis.

10. Abandonment Of Perfectionism

In some ways, the Pareto principle is the *antithesis* of perfectionism. It advocates shrugging off low-value activities and preoccupations. You're encouraged to focus on the 20% of actions that produces 80% of your results.

The 80/20 rule doesn't abide perfectionism. The latter has no place in a psyche that adheres to the former. If you struggle with perfectionism, I guarantee the Pareto principle will gradually whittle away that compulsion.

Bonus Benefit: Less Guilt

If you're spending a lot of time on things that aren't important to you, there's a good chance you're feeling guilty. Guilty for wasting your time. Guilty for doing so knowing that you could be using your time to achieve more rewarding goals. Guilty for feeling trapped in a cycle of ineffectiveness and unhappiness, and not knowing how to escape it.

The good news is that there's a simple solution: 80/20 your life. By applying the Pareto principle to every aspect of your day, you'll focus on the things that truly matter to you. The effects will be nearly instantaneous. From the work you create to the relationships you nurture, every choice you make will lead to a greater sense of fulfillment.

IN THE FOLLOWING SECTION, I'll take you on a brief tour of what we'll cover in *80/20 Your Life!* I have a feeling you're going to love what's coming your way.

WHAT YOU'LL LEARN IN 80/20 YOUR LIFE!

∼

As I mentioned earlier, most people talk about the 80/20 rule in the context of business. For example, 80% of sales comes from 20% of customers. Eighty percent of production comes from 20% of employees. Eighty percent of profit comes from 20% of products.

But the principle is directly applicable in every aspect of our lives. Moreover, the results are nothing short of extraordinary when we allow it to govern and guide our decisions.

This is the core tenet of *80/20 Your Life!* It forms the backbone of this book. To that end, I'll show you how to use the Pareto principle to optimize seven specific areas in your life.

Part 1: How To 80/20 Your Career

Whether you're searching for a new job or striving to advance your career at your current workplace, the 80/20 rule is a remarkable career development tool. From networking and zeroing in on the best opportunities to creating mentoring relationships and managing others, it can transform your professional life.

Part 1 will show you how to further your career without running yourself ragged in the process.

Part 2: How To 80/20 Your Home Life

There's no end to the list of things you need to do when you're at home. Cooking, vacuuming, dusting, sweeping, washing clothes, paying the bills, mowing the lawn, managing appointments, planning birthday parties, taking the kids to after-school activities, buying groceries, etc. It's easy to feel overwhelmed!

Part 2 will show you how to use the 80/20 rule to manage the workload and minimize your stress.

Part 3 : How To 80/20 Your Relationships

Your relationships should *enrich* your life, not detract from it. You should look forward to seeing your friends and loved ones, not dread their company. If you find yourself constantly complaining about certain people, it's time to do some pruning.

Part 3 will show you how to focus on the people in your life who embody the types of relationships you want to pursue.

Part 4: How To 80/20 Your Diet And Exercise Routine

Losing weight and getting into shape are difficult undertakings, even if you're fully committed to them. They're demanding in ways that discourage resolve. That's the reason so many people give up.

But what if you could get 80% of the way to your desired weight and physique with only 20% of the effort? Part 4 will show you how to use the 80/20 rule to streamline your diet and fitness routine.

Part 5: How To 80/20 Your Finances

Are you sick of tracking your expenses each week? Is your monthly budget overly complicated given what you're trying to accomplish? Do you feel flummoxed whenever you think about investing in stocks, bonds, and mutual funds?

Part 5 will show you how to reorganize your financial life so that it requires minimal time and attention.

Part 6: How To 80/20 Your Education And Training

Whether you're studying for an exam, learning a new language, or broadening your professional skillset, you can accelerate the process. The key is to use an approach that complements your brain's ability to absorb new information. The Pareto principle is the perfect learning tool.

Part 6 will show you how to apply this principle to learn things faster with better retention.

Part 7: How To 80/20 Your Small Business

Starting and running a small business requires a significant amount of time and focus. There are many moving parts that demand attention. From hiring talented people and creating a marketing strategy to pursuing leads and boosting profits, the small business owner's work is never done.

Part 7 will show you how to apply the 80/20 rule to your business. Whether you're outgrowing your office space or running a side gig from a corner of your bedroom, you'll discover how to leverage your time and resources so they have the greatest impact.

WE HAVE a lot of material to cover. But we're going to move fast. *80/20 Your Life!* isn't burdened with useless theories. It's filled with actionable advice arising from my personal experience.

Before we get started, let me make a few suggestions on how to make the most of the advice given throughout *80/20 Your Life!*

HOW TO GET MAXIMUM VALUE FROM THIS BOOK

~

First, don't get bogged down by the numbers 80 and 20. The relationship between inputs and outputs - or actions and results - is sometimes 65/35 and sometimes 95/5. The actual numbers matter little. Instead, focus on the *principle* behind the distribution: a minority of inputs is responsible for a majority of outputs.

In other words, focus on leverage.

Second, I strongly encourage you to do the work. The only way for this book to impact your daily experience is if you implement the advice. Merely reading *80/20 Your Life!* is not enough. Personal transformation can only occur if you apply what you read.

Third, take plenty of notes. I give a lot of examples

throughout this book. These examples are laden with tips and suggestions. But you're bound to think of your own ways to apply the advice according to your personal circumstances. Don't let these ideas evaporate. Write them down so you can take action on them later.

Fourth, be an active reader. Don't simply trust everything I say in *80/20 Your Life!* Rather, evaluate the relevance of my advice according to your needs and what you'd like to accomplish.

This is going to be a personal journey. I'll share what worked for me, and suggest practices that have worked for others. But ultimately, this journey is about you. Test everything. Treasure what works for you and discard the rest.

What This Book Is TRULY About

80/20 Your Life! isn't a playbook. It doesn't offer step-by-step instructions that guide you through every scenario you'll confront during the course of a given day. Rather, it's laden with real-life examples that illustrate the universal applicability of the Pareto principle.

My hope is that you'll see this principle at work in all aspects of your life. Some of the examples I'll provide will be immediately relevant to challenges you're dealing with right now. But even the examples that are less relevant to you are valuable. They demonstrate that the 80/20 rule can be applied in any situation and yield remarkable results.

It's my sincere hope that *80/20 Your Life!* will show you

the power you possess with regard to the decisions you make each and every day.

You're The CEO Of Your Life

A CEO's job is to decide an organization's strategic direction, monitor how his or her company is performing toward that end, and make adjustments accordingly. He or she is responsible for the organization's success.

Think of yourself as the CEO of your life. You have the same responsibilities as a corporate CEO. The difference is that you're focused on improving your quality of life. You're in charge of your happiness, financial picture, health, and personal growth. The buck stops with you.

This mindset clears away the useless drama and extraneous details that would otherwise hamper your success. You can instead focus your energy on leveraging your resources so they'll deliver the greatest impact.

That premise lies at the heart of *80/20 Your Life!*

You'll notice that this book is short. That's by design. Getting maximum value requires that you apply the advice and evaluate the results.

That's your job as the CEO of your life.

Now, let's roll up our sleeves and jump in...

PART I

HOW TO 80/20 YOUR CAREER

~

If you're like most people, your career takes up the majority of your waking hours. You spend a lot of time at your workplace. In some ways, your workplace may even seem like a second home. Even when you're not there, you're thinking about your responsibilities.

You care about your career. It not only provides you the means to live and afford the things you desire, but gives you a sense of accomplishment. It's more than a paycheck. Your work gives you *purpose*.

Naturally, you'd like to advance your career. Again, it's not about the money, although the further you advance, the more you'll earn. Nor is it about adding a shiny new title to your name. Rather, it's about devoting yourself to work that matters to you and gives you a sense of gratification. It's about investing in yourself, where the return on investment is most likely to be astronomical.

The problem is, with limited time and attentional resources, there's only so much you can do to develop your career. Therefore, it's important that you use your time wisely.

This section of *80/20 Your Life!* will examine three aspects of your career. I'll show you practical ways to use the Pareto principle to streamline and accelerate your career development.

STREAMLINE YOUR JOB SEARCH

~

Searching for a new job can become a full-time job in and of itself. Consider all of the activities involved with a typical job hunt:

You need to identify the best opportunities given your experience and skillset. You need to contact prospective employers and schedule interviews. You need to attend the interviews and follow up afterward. And that's just the beginning. There are a myriad of other tasks, such as getting your resume in order, lining up your referrals, cleaning up your social media, and attending networking events.

In short, the hunt for a new position can be a long, frustrating road. Whether you're seeking your first job after graduating college or searching for a new job while currently employed, it's important that you leverage your time.

That means focusing on the few tasks that'll have the greatest impact. In other words, use the 80/20 rule to decide how to best allocate your time and attention. Following are a few examples.

Apply To Positions That Fit Your Background

This might seem like a no-brainer to you. But you'd be surprised by how many people needlessly spin their wheels pursuing jobs that are unsuitable for them. That wastes time. Plus, it dilutes their effectiveness because they're not focusing on the opportunities that carry the greatest potential for success.

First, zero in on the positions that match your qualifications.

Second, identify the employers who are currently hiring for those positions.

Third, tailor your cover letter for those specific employers.

Forget the rest. The Pareto principle advises casting a narrow net. By focusing on the 20% of positions for which you're perfectly suited, your background and skills will outshine other candidates.

Network With People Who Can Help You

Many folks take an all-inclusive approach to networking. They seek to meet anyone and everyone in the hopes that someone can help them. They reason that the more people they talk to, the greater their chances of finding a promising opportunity.

This plan seems sensible at first. But in reality, it's likely to result in *missed* opportunities.

It's unwise to connect with everyone because doing so is usually a waste of valuable time. Sure, there's a chance that your second cousin's friend has an acquaintance that may be able to talk to someone at his company about an open position. But these prospects rarely pan out. You're better off using the 80/20 rule when you network.

First, when you attend networking events, focus on the 20% of individuals you *know* are able to help you. Nurture those relationships.

Second, spend only 20% of your time talking about yourself. Spend 80% of your time listening to others. You'll make a better impression.

Third, invert the 80/20 rule when following up with new people you've met. Spend the majority of your time following up with the small number of high-value contacts.

Networking can consume all of your time if you allow it to do so. That being the case, it's worth establishing guidelines that govern how you allocate your time. The Pareto principle offers an elegant solution.

Create A Plan With High-Payoff Potential

It's tempting to start contacting prospective employers right off the bat. After all, they're the ones who can hire you, so why not get started as soon as possible?

But the truth is, you'll be better served spending a little time upfront formulating a high-impact job search plan. This is a great application of the 80/20 rule. By spending 20% of your time carefully laying the groundwork for a successful job hunt, you'll avoid wasting valuable time on dubious pursuits later. Your plan will guide you and give you a much greater chance of finding the position you truly desire.

First, identify the type of job you want. Be specific.

Second, set weekly goals. Determine how many resumes you'll send each week, how many interviews you'll schedule, and how many people you'll reach out to in your industry.

Third, select two or three high-potential job-search tools to use. Examples include industry-specific job websites, college alumni career services, and headhunting services.

Don't waste time tweaking your resume. Don't spend days coming up with the perfect elevator pitch. Focus on the 20% of job-search activities that'll deliver the position you want.

IN THE NEXT SECTION, we'll assume you're currently employed and happy with your job. I'll show you how to use the 80/20 rule to take full advantage of your most precious resource: time.

THE PARETO PRINCIPLE AS A TIME MANAGEMENT TOOL

～

Time management plays a critical role in advancing your career. Spend your time wisely and you'll be able to successfully handle your job responsibilities, take on new, interesting projects, and complete a surprising amount of important work along the way. Fail to manage your time and your performance will inevitably suffer as you become overwhelmed with competing demands.

If you want to improve your career, it's crucial that you work smarter rather than harder. You must leverage your time in a way that has the greatest impact on your productivity.

The 80/20 rule will help you. Here's how to use it to make your job easier.

Managing And Completing Your To-Do Lists

You've undoubtedly seen mile-long to-do lists. They serve as bona fide brain dumps that include every task that comes to the owner's mind. Perhaps you even maintain such a list yourself. I did so years ago, before designing my current task management system.

But here's the ugly truth: long to-do lists hurt our productivity. They actually prevent us from getting things done. Worse, they impede our ability to get *important* work done as nonessential tasks drain our available time and erode our focus.

I recommend using the 80/20 rule to whip your current to-do lists into shape.

First, limit the number of items on your daily to-do list to seven. If you can get away with five, do so. It's okay to maintain a brain-dump list. But your *daily* to-do list is something entirely different.

Second, only include high-value tasks on your daily list. Eighty percent of the tasks you'll be tempted to put on your list won't contribute to your goals. Focus on the 20% that will.

Third, use only one task management system. If you'd like to maintain your to-do lists online, your options include Todoist, Nozbe, Flock, Asana, Flow, Wunderlist, Toodledo, OmniFocus, Any.do, Trello, Producteev, Hitask, and others. Some are free while others charge a fee. Some are better suited for personal to-do lists while a few, such as Trello, are designed to support collaborative projects. The important thing is that you pick one that meets your needs and complements your style and *stick with it.*

Notice that optimizing your task management system is largely about chipping away at the unnecessary and focusing on the essential. This two-pronged practice is at the heart of the Pareto principle.

Deciding What Projects To Take On

It's easy to take on so many projects that you eventually become overburdened with work. The motivation is under-standable. You want to impress your boss with your ability to deliver. You want the heightened visibility that comes with high-profile projects. You want the opportunity to show people that you're a valuable asset.

But if you take too much onto your plate, your enthusiasm is almost certain to produce the opposite effect. You'll miss deadlines because there's too much work demanding your time and attention. The increased visibility, once assumed to be advantageous, will become detrimental. Your poor performance will ultimately cause others to question your reliability.

Clearly, none of these things help your career.

Use the 80/20 rule to choose projects that cast you in a favorable light while helping you avoid becoming overburdened with work.

First, before you accept a project, make sure it aligns with your strengths. You don't want to waste time learning new skills just so you'll be able to deliver. You should only take on projects you're qualified to handle.

Second, focus on projects that promise minimal roadblocks. For example, avoid those for which you're unable to identify the key stakeholders. Such ambiguity may prevent you from acquiring the resources you need to see a project through to its end.

Third, devote your time to projects that interest you. It's one thing to possess the required skillset. It's another thing entirely to be absorbed by a project to the extent that you look forward to working on it. That level of interest ensures you'll do a good job.

You may not be in a position to choose your desired projects. Instead, they're delegated to you. But that doesn't mean you're without options. You can still apply the 80/20 rule and come out on top.

Sit down with your boss and discuss your reservations regarding being overburdened with work. Detail your current workload, and explain how certain projects you've been delegated may be delivered late due to lack of time, skills, experience, etc. Then, identify one or two projects where you can really make a difference and sell yourself as the obvious choice to spearhead them.

Your boss wants you to succeed. After all, when you do so, you make him or her look good. Use that as an inducement to get the projects that'll help your career.

Checking Email, Voicemails, Texts

One of the first things I learned while working in corporate America was that few incoming messages actually warranted a response from me. I could disregard the majority of them without consequence. That allowed me to focus on the emails, voicemails, and IMs (instant messages) that truly demanded my attention.

The Pareto principle was instrumental in helping me separate the wheat from the chaff with regard to communication. Once I stopped treating each message with the same level of attention and importance, I found it easy to dismiss most of them without guilt.

To be sure, there were occasions, albeit rare, when someone would say, "Hey, I didn't hear back from you about my email." I'd reply, "Sorry. I didn't realize you needed a response. What did you need from me?" Posing that question would usually confirm that my response was indeed unnecessary.

You can - and should - likewise use the 80/20 rule to reduce the volume of emails, voicemails, and texts you respond to.

First, create a folder in your email app and label it "Requires Action/Response." Place all emails that demand your attention into this folder.

Second, pick two times during the day to clear out this folder. Be consistent with the times. If you decide to do it at noon, do it at noon each day.

Third, refrain from returning voicemails and texts unless they're urgent. In most cases, they won't be.

It'll take time to adjust your coworkers' expectations. They may be accustomed to receiving immediate responses to every message they send. But over time, they'll get used to your streamlined manner of communication. In fact, some of them may even adopt it themselves after witnessing your increased productivity!

USING THE 80/20 RULE AS A MANAGER

~

L eaders must prioritize if they hope to be effective. They must separate the critical from the trivial, and allocate their resources so they'll have the greatest effect.

If you're a manager, the Pareto principle should form the backbone of your approach to leadership. It can help you to achieve extraordinary results, and allow you to do so without running yourself and your team ragged. This principle can literally transform your managerial style, boosting your team's performance and productivity in the process.

Following are a few ideas for applying the 80/20 rule in your role as leader.

Identify Your Most Productive/Capable Employees

Your employees are your greatest asset. But they can also represent your biggest frustration. Your job is to give them the tools they need to do *their* jobs while removing roadblocks, and inspiring, encouraging, and supporting them when necessary.

The problem is, each employee possesses different skills, harbors different mindsets, and faces different challenges stemming from their personalities. Some may even have agendas that conflict with your own. You could literally spend all day managing people with little to show for it.

The 80/20 rule will make your job as a manager easier and simpler. It's a matter of observing your employees and being honest with yourself about their abilities and predilections.

First, as a general rule, 20% of your team members will produce 80% of your team's output. Identify the 20%. These individuals are your hyper performers.

Second, figure out what motivates your top performers. Pick one or two of the largest influencing factors and deliver them.

Third, provide additional training to your most productive employees. They're going to drive most of your team's output. Therefore, it makes sense to give them opportunities to broaden their knowledge and expand their skillsets.

The above may seem unfair to your low-performing team members. After all, we're encouraged to see all employees as equal. But the fact is, all employees are *not* equal. Recognizing those who perform best, and rewarding them accordingly, pays dividends. It'll help you to become a more effective manager who can be relied upon to deliver.

Identify Employees Who Cause The Most Problems

In the same way that 20% of your employees will be responsible for 80% of your team's productivity, 20% will cause 80% of the problems. This minority will make most of the mistakes, take most of the sick days, submit most of the complaints, and cause most of the disciplinary issues.

Part of being an exceptional manager involves identifying problem employees and getting rid of them if rehabilitation isn't an option. The 80/20 rule can help you achieve that end.

First, once you identify your most difficult team members, spend a bit of time documenting the problems you've observed. These include issues involving performance, discipline, and attendance. Documentation is critical in the event you decide to fire them.

Second, conduct monthly, or even weekly, performance reviews. These sessions will give you an opportunity to listen to your problem employees' grievances and provide feedback and coaching. The sessions can be short, yet still have a huge impact on morale and performance.

Third, spend 20% of your time with these individuals

listening to their complaints and providing constructive feedback and coaching.

Third, if you decide to fire a difficult employee, don't dawdle. Don't let the process drag. Instead, fire fast. Expediting the process will save significant time and allow the rest of your team to regain their momentum.

Identify Employees Who Need A Lot Of Attention

Some of your team members may be especially needy. They'll need constant praise and hand-holding to feel valued. And if they're prone to making poor decisions, they'll need ongoing coaching to become, and remain, effective.

The problem is, your time as a manager is limited and always in demand. You can't spend your day catering to the neediness of a few employees. At the same time, it's important to listen to them and offer feedback and guidance. It may even be worth your while to mentor these individuals if you believe they possess potential.

Here's how to apply the Pareto principle in this scenario.

First, reassure these team members that you're available and want to help them to succeed. But make clear that your availability is limited given the demands associated with your position. This simple reassurance can go a long way toward making them feel confident enough to be effective. Meanwhile, they're forced to acknowledge that you can't be expected to be at their beck and call.

Second, set aside specific time periods that you can devote to your needy employees. For example, set aside an hour on Mondays and Thursdays, and schedule 10-minute "meetings" with each individual. Use these sessions to listen to their needs.

Third, praise these individuals. It only takes a moment to recognize them for something they've done well. Meanwhile, the praise you give them will bolster their confidence and encourage them to continue performing at a high level.

The Pareto Principle And The Extraordinary Manager

Managing people is a constant challenge. Even if each member of your team is performing well, you'll face a never-ending stream of demands on your time and attention. Being a successful leader requires that you generate large outputs from small inputs.

You must leverage your best employees. You must also identify your problem employees and let them go when coaching and feedback fail to have a positive impact.

The Universal Applicability Of The 80/20 Rule

This section has focused on how to use the 80/20 rule to further your career in a variety of scenarios. We talked about using it when searching for a job, managing your time in the workplace, and leading others in the role of manager. But the most salient point is that the 80/20 rule has countless applications. When you apply it, the results are always positive.

This point will become increasingly clear as we delve into other aspects of your daily experience. In Part 2, we'll expand and deepen this underlying theme by taking a look at how the Pareto principle can optimize your home life.

PART II

HOW TO 80/20 YOUR HOME LIFE

~

The work never ends at home. From cleaning the bathrooms and paying the bills to cooking dinner and pulling weeds outside, there's always another task demanding your attention. No matter how much you manage to get done, there's always more to do right around the corner.

It's even worse if you have a full-time job. You work hard during the week only to spend your weekends doing *additional* work around the house.

But what if you could finish the majority of household chores with minimal time and effort? You'd have more time to relax. You'd experience less stress. And you could look forward to pursuing things you *want* to do rather than things you *have* to do.

The 80/20 principle is just as applicable at home as it is in the workplace. For example, 20% of the rooms in your home will host 80% of the foot traffic. You likely wear 20% of your wardrobe 80% of the time. And among all the meals you're able to prepare, you probably prepare 20% of them 80% of the time.

You can use this insight to leverage your time at home, getting more work done with less action. By doing so, you'll have more opportunities to kick up your feet and relax, confident that your household is in terrific shape. This section will give you a boatload of ideas for doing precisely that.

APPLY THE 80/20 RULE TO HOUSE CLEANING

~

House cleaning is one the most time-intensive chores. And the bigger your house, the more time it takes.

But this chore doesn't need to consume your day. The fact is, you can get 80% of the way to a clean home with 20% of the effort you might otherwise spend. All it takes is a slight change in mindset and the willingness to let go of obsessive tendencies.

Following are a few ways to apply the Pareto principle to your house cleaning and reap the benefits in a fraction of the normal time.

Limit Your Cleaning Time

You have limited time at your disposal. So it's important to make the best use of it. One tactic for doing so is to give yourself a predetermined amount of time for completing a task, and sticking to that time frame. Once your time is up, you consider the task finished.

I've mentioned Parkinson's law in a couple of my other books. It dovetails nicely with the 80/20 rule. This law states that "work expands to fill the time available for its completion." So if you give yourself five hours to clean your home, you'll take five hours. If you shorten the available time frame to two hours, you'll get everything done in two hours.

Here are a few ideas for using the 80/20 rule and Parkinson's law to dramatically boost your productivity while cleaning your home.

First, focus on the areas of your home that receive the most use. Your kitchen likely receives more foot traffic than your guest room. So clean the former and forget the latter (unless you're planning to host someone).

Second, set a time limit for each room. For example, allow 15 minutes to clean the kitchen, 10 minutes to clean each bathroom, and 5 minutes to sweep the porch. If you need to vacuum your carpets, give yourself 20 minutes. No more.

Third, get rid of stuff you no longer use nor need. We'll talk about this more in a few moments.

You'll find that these three steps will spur you to work

faster. After all, you're giving yourself limited time to get the job done. Will your home be spotless, ready to be profiled in the next issue of *Good Housekeeping*? No. But it'll look great to the casual eye. Plus, you'll have a lot more free time on your hands.

Accept That Good Is Good Enough

I used to be a perfectionist. This trait manifested in various ways, including the time I spent making sure my home looked immaculate. Today, I realize the hours I spent obsessing about keeping everything spick and span were wasted. After all, the facade only lasted a short while; I had to repeat the cleaning cycle each week to maintain the pretense of perfection.

I eventually had a light-bulb moment: when it came to house cleaning, "good" was good enough. My home didn't need to look perfect. No one expected it to be so, and no one noticed when it *was* so. So I began to apply the Pareto principle. Here's how:

First, I drastically shortened the time I spent on each cleaning-related task (i.e. I applied Parkinson's law). For example, I used to spend an hour and a half vacuuming every nook and cranny, moving furniture to get at the hard-to-reach places. Following my light-bulb moment, I gave myself 20 minutes to vacuum the entire house. (I used a timer to keep myself honest.)

Second, I began to spot-clean. I stopped waiting for "Cleaning Day." Instead, if I noticed the coffee table in my family room was dusty, I'd spend 30 seconds dusting it. If I noticed crumbs and other debris on the carpet near the front door, I'd spend 30 seconds vacuuming it up.

Third, I nurtured a "good enough" attitude toward house cleaning. This step might sound unimportant, but in truth it was the most important one for me. Once I gave myself permission to stop at 80%, I was able to abandon my previous obsession with maintaining an immaculate-looking home. It simply wasn't a priority anymore.

If you typically spend an inordinate amount of time cleaning your home, I encourage you to experiment with the three steps above. You may find, like me, that you'd rather have more free time than maintain a spotless home that few, if any, will notice.

Identify The 20% Of Your Possessions You Value Most

According to the Pareto principle, we derive most of our enjoyment from a small proportion of our possessions. This means we can get rid of most of our possessions without suffering a significant impact to our lifestyle.

The problem is, most of us feel an attachment to the things we own. That's why it's so difficult to throw them out. You've no doubt hemmed and hawed over whether to discard items, even though you've not used them in years. Everyone has.

If you'd like to declutter your home, the 80/20 rule will be your most powerful ally. Here's how to use it:

First, categorize all of your belongings into one of two

groups: things you *frequently* use and things you use *rarely* often. Do this for your clothes, shoes, kitchen appliances, DVDs, knickknacks, bed sheets and pillowcases, makeup, hair care products, condiments, etc. Then, throw out everything you've placed in the second group.

Second, scrutinize each item in the first group. Ask yourself whether it truly brings you happiness. In some cases, you'll find that you're using certain items out of habit rather than for a specific purpose. If so, discard them.

Third, whenever you're about to purchase something, consider whether it'll become one of the possessions you use 80% of the time. If not, resist the temptation to buy it. It'll only clutter your home.

This isn't about becoming a minimalist. Rather, it's about maintaining a clean living space in a fraction of the time you'd otherwise spend if you entertained a conventional mindset. The 80/20 rule is a lever that maximizes your effectiveness toward that end with minimal action.

USE THE PARETO PRINCIPLE TO SIMPLIFY COOKING

∾

C ooking takes as much time as you allow it. It's possible to spend hours in the kitchen preparing elaborate meals. It's also possible to spend a fraction of the time preparing simple meals that bring you just as much satisfaction.

Although I enjoy cooking, it's not a priority for me. Whenever possible, I try to minimize the time I spend preparing dishes. I'd rather spend that time reading, writing, or enjoying other leisure activities.

To this end, I use the 80/20 rule whenever I cook. If you'd like to spend less time in the kitchen, I recommend the following tactics.

Prepare Meals That Require Minimal Effort

Many recipes are complicated and difficult to master. Sure, the dishes taste great and can evoke admiration from your guests, but their preparation requires an exorbitant amount of time. For example, an expertly-prepared beef Wellington will impress even the most surly foodie, but is it worth spending hours to prepare it?

In my opinion, no. If you feel similarly, here's how you can streamline your cooking.

First, focus on dishes that require few ingredients. I recommend limiting the number of ingredients to five.

Second, collect easy recipes. Save them so you'll never be at a loss for dishes to prepare. And remember, easy doesn't have to mean boring. Countless meals are easy to make and will light up your taste buds.

Third, learn to love leftovers. That'll give you the freedom to prepare dishes you can enjoy night after night. And *that'll* cut down on preparation time. For example, a scrumptious beef stew will be just as tasty tomorrow night as it is tonight. The only difference is that you won't have to spend time preparing it tomorrow night.

The idea is to spend less time in the kitchen and still feel satisfied by the meals you've prepared.

Avoid Trendy, High-Maintenance Diets

Many diets take a lot of time and effort - and sometimes money - to maintain. For example, the 17-Day Diet, recommended by author and psychologist Dr. Phil, practically requires a notebook to keep track of everything. Worse, contrary to its name, the diet doesn't merely last 17 days. Each *cycle* of the diet lasts 17 days (there are four cycles).

This diet, although popular, is reportedly high-maintenance. And though it's in vogue, it's hardly necessary if you want to get into shape. If you're intent on following a diet, I recommend using the Pareto principle to pick one that won't overburden you with its complexity.

First, take a look at how the diet is organized. Note whether it requires you to follow a complicated daily regimen (e.g. eat food X on day 1, food Y on day 2, and food Z on day 3, and so forth). Also, note whether it follows an intricate points system, such as the one used by Weight Watchers. If either is the case, avoid it.

Second, consider whether the diet aligns with your lifestyle. If you enjoy the outdoors, don't hitch yourself to a diet that requires lengthy meal preparation or meals that must be kept refrigerated at all times.

Third, don't feel as if you must follow a particular diet to the letter. Be willing to cut corners if doing so will save you time without severely affecting the outcome. Being a stickler can backfire, prompting you to give up when you lack the motivation to continue. Concentrate on getting 80% of the way there.

Focus On Natural, Nutritional Foods

I'm not an advocate of dieting. Diets have always seemed to me like short-term solutions that deliver questionable long-term results. That is, you restrict your eating to certain foods for a specific time period, and once that period is over you can resume eating anything you like.

That approach has never resonated with me.

I prefer to stick to a simple way of eating that incorporates natural foods while restricting processed foods. This approach is consistent with the 80/20 rule. I'm able to follow a reasonably healthy meal plan without the time, effort, and overall hassle involved with following short-term diets.

In my opinion, it's a fine way to streamline cooking, thereby saving a lot of time and effort. Following are a few tips for applying the 80/20 rule in the context of eating simply.

First, focus on foods that offer nutrition. If a particular food offers no nutrition, refrain from including it in your meals. An example is white rice. It has zero nutritional value. So avoid wasting time preparing it.

Second, make a list of your favorite nutritional foods. Categorize them by type: fruits, vegetables, fish, chicken, etc. Doing this serves two purposes. It gives you something to reference when deciding what dishes to prepare. That way, you're never at a loss. It also streamlines the ingredients you'll use, simplifying your meals.

Third, make a list of your three favorite lunch dishes

and three favorite dinner dishes. These will be your go-to meals. It'll drastically reduce the number of potential meals you can prepare, which, in turn, will simplify decisions regarding what to eat.

Cooking doesn't have to consume much time if you're willing to cut out a lot of the unnecessary fluff. The Pareto principle is an invaluable aid toward that end.

ENJOY YOUR HOBBIES TO THEIR FULLEST POTENTIAL

~

Some folks have too many hobbies. An example is the fellow who aspires to be a master chef, a guitar virtuoso, a black belt in karate, an expert at archery, all while attempting to become a chess grandmaster. To say his plate of full is an understatement.

Other folks have no hobbies at all. They spend their time doing things that fail to make them happy in the long run, but do them out of habit. An example is the person who spends hours each day on social media, but feels a general sense of discontent.

Hobbies are an important part of a rewarding home life. They relieve stress, engage our minds, and help us to form connections with those who share our interests. If you're having trouble finding a hobby to pursue, you lack the time to pursue one, or you're feeling overwhelmed by too many hobbies, I encourage you to use the 80/20 rule. Here's how:

Limit Binge-Watching Television Shows

I understand the temptation. You come home after a hard day at your job and want nothing more than to vegetate in front of your television. Or maybe you're watching a captivating TV series, such as *Homeland* or *Broadchurch*, and persuade yourself (over and over) to watch "just one more episode."

Before you know it, several hours have passed and you have nothing to show for it. Worse, at the end of your binge-watching session, you feel more exhausted than ever. Some folks even experience situational depression, particularly when they finish a favored series.

Who can possibly think of hobbies in such a condition?

I recommend limiting what you watch on TV. Further, I recommend using the 80/20 rule to guide your decisions.

First, if you subscribe to multiple streaming services (Netflix, Hulu, etc.), pick one and cancel the others. I realize that might mean abandoning shows you enjoy, but that'll always be the case. There's no better time than the present to cut the cord.

Second, review the shows you watch. Rate them from one to ten in terms of how much you enjoy them. Abandon any shows that rate below eight.

Third, limit the amount of time you spend watching TV. U.S. adults watch an average of five hours per day. Over seven days, it's practically a full-time job. Commit to watching only two hours a day.

The point is to use the 80/20 rule to free up time you can use to pursue a couple hobbies. I'm willing to bet you'll barely miss most of the TV series you abandon.

Select Hobbies That Provide The Most Satisfaction

Your hobbies should be rewarding. Otherwise, there's no point in pursuing them. The challenge is, there are likely dozens of hobbies you'd enjoy. You can't pursue them all due to lack of time. So, you have to pick one or two that promise to deliver the best experience.

I encourage you to use the Pareto principle. Here are a few suggestions:

First, make a list of every activity you enjoy. Once you've completed this list, pick the five you enjoy the most.

Second, think about roadblocks that might prevent you from pursuing the five favored activities on your list. For example, you may enjoy skiing, but location and transportation might present problems. You might enjoy skydiving, but time and money may be limiting factors. Pick the two hobbies for which there are the fewest roadblocks.

Third, consider whether you need others to participate in the two hobbies that remain. For example, you need others to play poker, basketball, tennis, and billiards. But playing the guitar, cooking, gardening, and crossword puzzles? Those can be done on your own.

It's fine if one of your hobbies requires other people. But if it does, make sure the other hobby doesn't.

Combine Hobbies With Your Goals

The core of the 80/20 rule is getting maximum results from minimal action. A great way to achieve that outcome is to select hobbies that complement your goals. Doing so produces multiple positive effects while expending your time and energy toward a single pursuit. In other words, you get more bang for your buck.

First, make a list of your goals. This might include running a full marathon, meeting new people, and building muscle mass.

Second, think of hobbies that align with these goals. For example, jogging complements your desire to run a marathon. Attending Meetup events is a great way to meet new people who share your interests. Weight training supports your aim to build muscle mass.

Third, choose two hobbies from your list. Start with two to avoid overburdening yourself, and if time permits add a third down the road.

By combining your hobbies with your goals, you'll increase your results without increasing the time you spend pursuing them.

That's what the Pareto principle is all about.

Can You Turn Your Hobby Into A Business?

Suppose you'd like to start a side business to generate extra income. Running a business, even a small one, takes a lot of time and energy. Why not leverage your use of these resources by turning one of your hobbies into a business?

For example, if you enjoy making jewelry, why not sell it on Etsy, eBay, or via Shopify? You can do the same thing with painting, throwing pottery, and making candles. If you enjoy photography, why not offer your services to your friends and family members? If you enjoy baking, start a side gig making baked goods and decorating cakes.

The point is to leverage your time. Take an activity you enjoy doing, and would likely do for free, and charge money for your expertise.

First, make a list of hobbies you can do on your own. These are activities you can enjoy without needing other people to participate.

Second, brainstorm products and services you can deliver while pursuing these hobbies (e.g. handmade jewelry, baked goods, family portraits, etc.).

Third, identify the hobby that offers the simplest and easiest path to the market. That's your ideal hobby, at least in the context of starting a side business.

If you don't currently have a hobby, I encourage you to pick one. If you have too many, I encourage you to let some of them go. The "trick" to enjoying your favorite activities to their fullest is to make sufficient time for them and focus on a few to the exclusion of all others.

In other words, apply the 80/20 rule.

MAKE THE MOST OF YOUR LEISURE TIME

~

Free time. There's never enough of it, and the little we enjoy evaporates too quickly. So it's important to make the most of the free time we have at our disposal.

The question is, how do we measure the value of leisure time? How do we determine whether we're spending it wisely?

The answers are going to be unique to each of us. Personally, I want to spend my free time in ways that maximize my quality of life. It's not just about relaxing after a tough day. I want to get as much mileage as possible from the leisure activities I pursue.

The Pareto principle has been instrumental in helping

me to optimize how I spend my free time. I'm confident it can serve you in that same regard.

Below are four things you can do starting today to enjoy more of what life has to offer while taking less action.

Stop Reading Novels You No Longer Enjoy

Long ago, I felt strange abandoning books before I had finished reading them. Part of me kept hoping the books would get better. But a larger part simply felt guilty about tossing them aside. I'd tell myself, "Don't be a quitter. Finish the book!" And I'd reluctantly pick it back up and keep reading.

I now recognize this to be an act of folly. In my opinion, life is too short to read books I don't enjoy. After all, completing such books prevents me from moving on to others I'll find more rewarding.

The 80/20 rule suggests that 20% of the books we read will be responsible for 80% of our enjoyment. That's a diplomatic way of saying 80% of the books we read will be a waste of time. With that in mind, here's how to use the 80/20 rule to streamline your fiction reading.

First, select novels that dovetail with your interests. If you enjoy science fiction, don't pick up a literary fiction novel. If you prefer psychological thrillers, don't pick up a satire. You might ultimately enjoy literary fiction and satire, but unless you specifically intend to explore a new genre, it makes sense to stick to your preferences.

Second, commit to jumping ship at the 25% mark if a

book fails to engage you. If you don't find a book engaging after a quarter of the way, you're unlikely to find it engaging later. You might, but you're better off cutting your losses and moving on.

Third, when you find a novelist you enjoy, stick with him or her. Read everything written by that author. I've found that if I love one novel by a particular author, I'll probably enjoy his or her other novels.

The key is to cut through the chaff and zero in on the 20% of books that are likely to deliver most of your reading enjoyment. Of course, you should experiment with unfamiliar authors and explore unfamiliar genres. But for *most* of your reading, stick to what works for you.

Create A Strategy For Reading Non-Fiction Books

I read quite a bit of non-fiction, most of which is in the personal development field. Over the years, I've settled on a strategy for reading such books in a way that allows me to get the most out of them.

In my opinion, there's a right way and a wrong way to read non-fiction. The right way follows the 80/20 rule, and I wholeheartedly recommend you try it.

First, as with novels, don't feel as if you must finish a book. Toss it aside if it doesn't interest you. Move on to a book you find to be more useful, engaging, or insightful.

Second, scan the table of contents before you begin to read the book. Look for items that are immediately relevant to you. Again, don't feel like you have to read the entire book. It's okay to skip to the relevant sections. The table of contents will also provide a roadmap. You'll be able to see where the author is starting, his or her destination, and how he or she intends to get there.

Third, highlight important passages. If you're reading a print book, use a yellow highlighter. If you're reading the book on a Kindle or phone, use the highlighting feature. Come back to these passages later for reminders or to glean new insights from them.

You read non-fiction to learn. Use the Pareto principle to learn the *important* material as quickly as possible.

Spend Less Time Aimlessly Surfing The Internet

I'm convinced the internet is one of the biggest impediments to our sustained focus and productivity. It's like a giant slot machine where each visit to a website is like the pull of the slot's arm. We hope for a payout, which, in this case, takes the form of intriguing content (celebrity news, social media arguments, etc.).

The brain considers finding such content to be like winning a small jackpot. Consequently, dopamine floods the brain and encourages us to pull the slot's arm again.

And this happens over and over, making it increasingly difficult to break the cycle.

This is no way to spend leisure time. It may seem gratifying in the moment, but ultimately leaves an empty feeling behind. If you suspect your free time is being commandeered by your internet habits, use the 80/20 rule to curtail your activity.

First, make a list of the 20 websites you visit most often during the week. Then, note the amount of time you spend on each one. If you're unable to come up with accurate estimates, use RescueTime or a similar time tracking app to monitor your online activity.

Second, circle five sites on your list that you'll allow yourself to visit in the future. These will likely be the sites at which you spend the majority of your time.

Third, set a timer for 60 minutes at the beginning of each day. Start the timer each time you visit one of these five sites. Allow it to count down, and only stop it when you stop surfing. Continue to do this throughout the day without resetting the timer. When the timer finally reaches zero, you'll have effectively used up that day's web surfing time.

These three tactics will drastically reduce the amount of leisure time you spend online. That'll free up the time so you can use it toward more productive and rewarding pursuits. This might include taking classes that cater to your interests, spending time with your loved ones, and improving yourself by learning new skills.

In The Workplace, At Home, And Everywhere

As effective as the 80/20 rule is in the workplace, it's just as effective at home. Indeed, when it comes to realizing bigger results from less action, the 80/20 rule is applicable everywhere.

In the next section, we'll turn our attention to relationships. You'll discover the Pareto principle can improve the quality of your social life, family life, and love life in surprising ways.

PART III

HOW TO 80/20 YOUR RELATIONSHIPS

~

Personal connections are vital to our quality of life. The bonds we share with our friends and loved ones make us feel valued. They give us a sense of security and comfort. When we're dealing with difficult issues, it's helpful simply to be near those we trust to support and encourage us.

Our relationships enrich our lives, sometimes in ways that are as subtle as they are pivotal to our happiness. So it's important to nurture them.

Unfortunately, many people have allowed their most significant relationships to erode due to inattention. Social media has bamboozled folks into believing their online relationships are just as rich and textured as those they enjoy in person.

In truth, they're not. Our online friends can keep us company, entertain us with gossip, and chat about popular movies and TV shows. But they don't truly know us. At least, not in the way our real-life friends know us.

Is it any wonder we're feeling more isolated than ever before despite having constant access to "friends" online?

Most of us could benefit from devoting more attention to our social lives. Feeling happy and content isn't the result of having a *lot* of relationships. It stems from cultivating and nurturing the *right* relationships.

I'll show you how to use the Pareto principle to focus on the connections that matter.

OPTIMIZE THE TIME YOU SPEND WITH LOVED ONES

~

We often take our loved ones for granted. Maybe not everyday, and certainly not on purpose, but we do so all the same. The continued presence of our spouses and children give us a perception of permanence. They're always there, and we assume they'll always be so.

Consequently, our attention to these central relationships wanes. It's human nature. We focus on things we fear we might lose. The irony is that, in doing so, we often fail to nurture the most important relationships in our lives.

If you suspect the bonds you share with your loved ones have frayed, now's the time to strengthen them. Below, I'll show you how to use the 80/20 rule to make these crucial connections your top priority.

Be Purposeful

It's easy to fall into the comfortable rhythm of reacting to our families' needs. For example, if our spouses require our help, we offer it. When our children engage us, we respond to them.

This tendency makes us feel as if we're helping our families to thrive. But in reality, it merely allows them to tread water. Meanwhile, the sense of familiarity slowly whittles away the unique, emotional connection we feel towards them.

Perhaps you've heard friends complain that they feel as if their spouses have become like roommates and their children like tenants. That's what happens when we fail to give our loved ones the purposeful attention they deserve.

The good news is, we can easily turn things around by applying the Pareto principle.

First, recognize that 80% of your interactions with your family are trivial. They don't count as quality time. Such interactions are usually incidental and do nothing to reinforce the connections you share with your spouse and kids. An example is asking your spouse whether he or she paid the mortgage. Another example is asking your kids whether they finished their homework.

Second, be purposeful when you communicate with your family. It's easy to give short, glib answers to questions asked by your loved ones. For example, when asked "how was your day," you reply "fine." Instead, take the time to answer thoughtfully with details. And when you ask your loved ones about their days, listen attentively. The better your communication, the deeper the connection.

Third, plan activities that you and your loved ones will enjoy together. For example, go on weekly dates with your spouse. If your kids are young, take them to the park and play with them a few times a week. If they're older, organize a weekly outing - for example, visit local museums, go fishing, or go on hikes. Or stay home and play board games together.

Twenty percent of your interactions with your loved ones do the heavy lifting when it comes to cementing the bonds you share with them. Rather than allowing these interactions to happen haphazardly, be purposeful. It takes time and effort, but pays dividends that make the investment worthwhile.

Ignore Your Phone

In my opinion, our phones represent one of the biggest threats to families' quality time. We've become accustomed to carrying them with us at all times. They're our primary means of connecting with the world around us, and we constantly put them to use.

The downside is that our phones dominate our attention. We instinctively reach for them whenever we receive a text, email, or call. We do it while having dinner with our families. We do it in the middle of important conversations. We do it when we're at restaurants, in theaters, and even while camping.

We seem unable to resist the impulse to check our phones, much like Pavlov's dogs were unable to resist drooling at the sound of a dinner bell.

If your phone has this power over you, it's likely impacting your family. Here's how to use the 80/20 rule to resist its siren call.

First, realize that 80% of the messages you receive are unimportant. Perhaps even 90%. They can be ignored without consequence.

Second, based on the above, commit to turning your phone off whenever you spend quality time with your family. The odds of receiving a truly urgent message that warrants interrupting this time are infinitesimal. Play the odds.

Third, ask your family to do the same. Encourage them to think of the times you spend together as "no-phone zones."

Ignore 80% Of The Things That Annoy You

As much as we love and adore our spouses and kids, they regularly annoy us. It doesn't feel good to admit it, but it's true. (Likewise, you can assume you regularly annoy them, too.)

Maybe you disapprove of your spouse leaving unwashed dishes in the sink. Perhaps you silently grouse when your children leave trash between the sofa cushions. Or maybe your family habitually tracks mud on the carpets despite your repeated requests for them to take their shoes off while in the house.

It's difficult to appreciate our loved ones when we're irritated with them. For that reason, I recommend using the Pareto principle to control your annoyance.

First, figure out why you get annoyed. Often, the reasons have little to do with the person whose actions annoy us. Much of our irritation stems from our immediate circumstances. For example, if you've just spent 90 minutes in bumper-to-bumper traffic, you're more likely to be annoyed than if you had been relaxing at home with an engaging novel and glass of your favorite wine. If you're already on edge, think twice before blaming the person at whom you're annoyed.

Second, recognize that 80% of the things that annoy us are inconsequential. They're small things that matter little. Treat them as such. For example, rather than becoming annoyed at the sight of unwashed dishes in the sink, spend 60 seconds washing them. Forgive and move on.

Third, remind yourself that "this too shall pass." This practice may seem silly, but consider this: we usually become annoyed in the heat of the moment. Something happens that we dislike, and we immediately get upset. This is an emotional response, not one born of rational thought. When you tell yourself "this too shall pass," you recognize the temporary nature of whatever is irking you. Most of the things that irk us are trivial, short-lived, and therefore not worth our irritation.

STRENGTHEN BONDS YOU SHARE WITH (GOOD) FRIENDS

~

Most of us have too many friends. Perhaps it's more accurate to say we have too many acquaintances whom we convince ourselves are our friends. The end result is the same. We spend too much of our limited time maintaining friendships that are unimportant to us.

The problem is, the more time we spend on these questionable friendships, the less time we have to devote to the ones that truly make us happy. That being the case, it's worth cutting back.

The 80/20 rule is a useful tool for identifying friends to whom you should allocate most of your time and focus.

Identify The 20% Of Your Friends With Whom You Spend 80% Of Your Time

You probably spend most of your time with a relatively small number of friends. For example, you may have 100 friends, but spend 80% of your time with 20 of them. This doesn't mean you *should* be spending the majority of your time with these 20 friends. We're just noting that you're doing so.

Before you can nurture your most important friendships, the ones you find most rewarding, you need to know who you're currently spending time with. Here's how:

First, make a list of your top 100 friends.

Second, note how much time you spend with each of them on a monthly basis. Include time spent in person as well as time spent on the phone and sending texts and emails.

Third, identify good friends who are receiving significantly less time from you than friends who offer less value (we'll talk more about this below).

Pare Down The Number Of Friendships You're Trying To Maintain

Many people feel that they're failing to keep in adequate contact with their friends. They complain that their friendships are slowly slipping away from them due to inattention.

One of the most common causes of this situation is the tendency to maintain too many friendships. Their time is divided in too many directions, leaving little to spend where it'll yield the most rewarding results.

If you're in this predicament, the solution is to whittle down the number of friendships you're trying to maintain. Here are a few suggestions:

First, determine how much time you have available to spend with friends. If you work full-time and have a large family, you'll have less time available than a single twenty-something who works part-time.

Second, refer to the list of your top 100 friends (or however many friends you have). You can probably sever at least half of those connections without consequence. These are the "friends" with whom you spend little time, share scant intimacy, and have little in common with.

Third, refrain from reaching out to the half (or more) you've identified as expendable. This may seem insensitive. And in truth, it is. But it's necessary to give you the freedom to pursue the friendships that matter most to you. It may console you to know that those relationships are probably just as important to them as they are to you, which is to say not important at all.

Focus Your Time On The Most Rewarding Friendships

The final step is to create an "A" list of friends. This list will include the folks you trust with your secrets. They're the friends you know will look out for your interests and support you in times of need. They're the ones who will help you through the bad times, and root you on and celebrate your triumphs.

If you're like most people, you can count the number of such friends on one hand. That's good news since your time is limited. The problem is, unless you've taken the time to identify them, you may not know who they are. Here's how to fix that problem.

First, write down all of the characteristics you value. Don't be timid. Pretend as if you're creating the ultimate friend.

Second, review your abridged list of friends from above. This is your top 100 list sans the relationships you consider to be expendable.

Third, appraise each person on the list. Consider how many of your favored characteristics he or she possesses. Assign each friend a score from one to ten on this basis.

This exercise may seem tactless. But it's a practical way to identify the friends you enjoy the most. You may discover that a friend with whom you've been spending a lot of time isn't the type of friend you value. It's better to know this upfront. That way, you can make a rational decision regarding whether to continue that relationship.

When our friendships align with our values, needs, experiences, and expectations, we feel more satisfied. Yet, many of us have a tendency to focus our time and attention on situational friendships - those stemming from circumstance.

The Pareto principle helps us cut through the fog. It

gives us a way to identify who brings us the most joy so we can nurture those connections, giving them the time and attention they deserve.

THE 80/20 RULE OF MEETING NEW PEOPLE

~

I t's not difficult to meet new people. The challenge is deciding which of these folks are worth pursuing as friends. As proposed by the 80/20 rule, quality trumps quantity. And so we want to be able to sift through the crowds and gravitate toward people whose personalities, values, and experiences align with our own.

This isn't about seeking "perfect" friends. There *are* no perfect friends. Rather, it's about evaluating the people you meet and identifying those who are most likely to have a positive, rewarding, and long-term impact in your life.

We'll use the Pareto principle to guide us.

Don't Try To Become Friends With Everyone You Meet

It's one thing to be approachable and friendly to new people. It's another thing entirely to assume each new person will become a close confidante.

People are generally on their best behavior when you meet them for the first time. Given that, your first impression of them may stem from a facade. There's no way to know for certain, even if you're adept at reading people.

So we must have a way to determine relatively quickly whether strangers will eventually make true friends. Most won't, but a few will.

The 80/20 rule will help us to save time. It gives us a guideline to use when appraising the potential of new friendships.

First, recognize that the majority of people you meet will not become true friends. The odds are simply against it. The older we get, the more importance we place on our values and convictions. The odds of strangers' values and convictions dovetailing with our own are small, and grow slimmer as we age.

Second, with the above in mind, be willing to abandon new relationships that seem to blossom but hold little long-term potential. You'll find that this circumstance prevails among the majority of the people you encounter.

Third, always remain approachable. Even though most new relationships quickly fizzle, you might meet someone that eventually becomes a great friend. I experienced this a few years ago. I met a fellow at a coffeeshop, and discovered we shared the same values, experiences, and goals. Today, he's a big part of my social life. It's rare, but it happens.

Focus Your Time On Folks Who Complement Your Personality

We tend to get along best with people who have personalities that complement our own. That's not to say they're mirror images of us. Nor is it to suggest they have the *same* personalities. Rather, their dominant traits dovetail nicely with ours.

For example, consider the Myers-Briggs personality type indicator.[1] It identifies 16 distinct personality types. One of them is labeled ISTJ, which stands for introversion (I), sensing (S), thinking (T), judgment (J). People with this personality type are considered to be practical, organized, and responsible. While ISTJs tend to get along well with other ISTJs, they also complement several other personality types. Their dominant traits differ, but dovetail with, the dominant traits of these other types.

When you meet new people, pay particular attention to their personalities. You'll be able to glean *some* insight from their remarks. But much more insight can be gained by asking specific questions.

Once again, we can use the 80/20 rule to streamline our efforts.

First, familiarize yourself with the 16 personality types defined by the Myers-Briggs personality type indicator.

Note which type you are, and observe which types align with you. This will help you to weed out much of the field.

Second, look for dominant traits of complementary personality types. For example, suppose your type is ISTJ. You tend to get along well with ESTPs, which stands for extraversion (E), sensing (S), thinking (T), perception (P). Dominant traits include good situational awareness, forthright communication, and deep engagement during conversation. As an ISTJ, you're likely to be compatible with someone who possesses these attributes.

Third, refrain from spending significant time with those who have non-complementary personality types. For example, according to the Myers-Briggs personality type indicator, ISTJs are less compatible with INFPs, which stands for introversion (I), intuition (N), feeling (F), perception (P). If you recognize the dominant traits of an INFP in a stranger, you can save yourself time by limiting your interaction with him or her.

The Myers-Briggs indicator isn't the last word on compatibility between select personalities. But it's a convenient tool the use of which is consistent with the 80/20 rule.

Create Filters To Identify Promising "Candidates"

Thus far, we've talked about limiting the number of strangers you try to befriend and using personality types to make this process easier (or at least more systematized). Using the Myers-Briggs type indicator is one way - and a terrific one at that - to filter candidates. But there are additional filters you can use to improve the odds that you spend time with potential friends you'll enjoy for years to come.

This practice, like using the Myers-Briggs type indicator, is yet another way to take advantage of the Pareto principle when meeting new people.

First, make a list of personality traits you dislike. Examples include being argumentative, self-absorbed, or prone to gossiping behind others' backs.

Second, rank each trait on a scale of one to ten according to how obnoxious and unpleasant you find it.

Third, use this list to decide whether someone you've met is worth pursuing as a friend.

For example, suppose you're an ISTJ on the Myers-Briggs type indicator. You normally get along well with ESTPs. But let say you meet an ESTP who comes across as selfish, arrogant, and close-minded. You happen to abhor these three traits. That being the case, you should trust your filters rather than relying solely on the compatibility matches of the Myers-Briggs type indicator.

It's a great way to apply the 80/20 rule toward finding people you'll truly connect with throughout your life.

[1] http://www.myersbriggs.org/my-mbti-personality-type/mbti-basics/

APPLY THE PARETO PRINCIPLE TO DATING

~

Have you ever gone on a string of unsuccessful dates and wondered why things turned out poorly? Perhaps you blamed yourself, allowing your inner critic to point out imaginary flaws. Maybe you blamed your dates, convinced they were moody, reserved, or sarcastic.

The truth is, the dates were likely doomed from the start. You were just going out with people who weren't a good match for you.

As in other areas of your life where challenges arise due to limited resources and competing demands, there's an easy solution: use the 80/20 rule. It'll help you to decide who to go out with and when to cut your losses. To that end, it'll prevent you from wasting valuable time pursuing relationships that hold little long-term promise.

Prioritize Quality Over Quantity

If you're dating to find the one person who's right for you, it's tempting to go on as many dates as possible.

That's the principle behind speed dating. The idea is that the more people you meet and interact with, the greater your chances of finding a great match. So you meet dozens of potential partners within a short period and spend a few minutes getting to know each of them.

The problem is, three to five minutes isn't enough time to determine whether the person you're talking to has potential as a long-term partner. In fact, research suggests that being presented with such a wide array of dating options does nothing to improve our emotional satisfaction. [1] Indeed, the more options in front of us, the more difficulty we have choosing between them.[2]

In other words, less may indeed be more.

This idea, of course, dovetails perfectly with the Pareto principle. For this reason, I encourage you to use it when deciding whom to date.

First, before you agree to go out on a date, ask yourself whether you like the person or if you're just feeling lonely. If the latter case is true, say no to the date. Otherwise, you'll be tempted to see the individual as a cure for loneliness rather than a potential long-term partner.

Second, be clear about what you want from a relationship. Write down the five attributes that are most important to you. Use them as a baseline to filter potential dates.

Third, ask questions. Find out what matters to the person. Learn about his or her interests and goals. Yes, you'll want to talk about these things in greater detail if you decide to go on a date with the person. But asking upfront, if only to get a general sense of him or her, will help you to decide whether going on a date is worthwhile in the first place.

According to the Pareto principle, 80% of your enjoyment while dating will come from 20% of your dates. So it pays to focus on quality over quantity.

Create A List Of Deal Breakers

We usually focus on the traits we'd like to see in our dating partners. Examples include being open, kind, and empathetic. We hope the other person has a sense of humor, a strong moral compass, and plans for the future. This is important because it helps us to qualify people in the context of pursuing meaningful relationships with them.

Having said that, it's equally important to think about the characteristics we abhor. Examples include dishonesty, narcissism, rudeness, and a terrible temper. These traits are deal breakers. We benefit by steering clear of potential partners who exhibit them.

Using deal breakers as a dating filter is an excellent application of the 80/20 rule. Saying no to people you're unlikely to enjoy will allow you to more quickly find people you *will* enjoy.

First, make a list of your personal deal breakers. Although some traits are universally unappealing (e.g. dishonesty), others will be unique to your sensibilities. An example might be tobacco use or a penchant for alcohol.

Second, before you agree to go on a date, find out whether your potential dating partner exhibits any of these deal breakers. Ask direct questions if necessary.

Third, if you notice highly-undesirable traits, be willing to say no to a date, even if you like other things about the person. You won't be able to ignore attributes you find objectionable in the long run.

Note that deal breakers are distinct from pet peeves. The latter are simply things that irk us. The former are things we find highly offensive, and thus cannot tolerate.

Use The 80/20 Rule When Setting Expectations

It's natural to have expectations when we go out on dates. We expect the people we date to be open, well-mannered, and curious about us enough to ask questions.

But often, our expectations extend further than the dates themselves. For example, we might worry whether our dating partners will fit in with our friends. We may stew over the exclusivity of the blossoming relationship. Or we might think about whether our families will get along.

Having expectations is good. But it's important to make sure they're realistic and not get ahead of ourselves. Use the Pareto principle to zero in on *relevant* expectations that'll help you decide whether to go on another date with the person.

First, write down your expectations. Then, review each one and ask yourself whether it's reasonable. For example, you might expect your date to remember every detail you tell him or her about your life. But unless the person has demonstrated a perfect memory, that expectation is probably unjustified. Cross off all such expectations from your list.

Second, rate the remaining expectations according to how important they are to you. Assign each a value from one to ten with one signifying those that are the most important.

Third, focus only on the expectations you rated with a one.

Successful dating isn't about finding the perfect partner. It's about identifying and spending your time with the ones who show the greatest potential. To do that, you must have a way to filter the majority. The 80/20 rule makes this process a snap.

[1] http://www.indiana.edu/~abcwest/pmwiki/pdf/lenton.ieee.2008.pdf

[2] http://rsbl.royalsocietypublishing.org/content/early/2011/02/24/rsbl.2011.0098

PART IV

HOW TO 80/20 YOUR DIET AND EXERCISE ROUTINE

~

Diet and exercise can be as complicated as you make them. You've undoubtedly heard about the convoluted meal and workout regimens many people adhere to in the pursuit of weight loss and general fitness. They eat certain foods, or focus on certain macronutrients, on certain days. They follow intricate workout routines that string together a long list of exercises, each designed to focus on a specific area of their bodies.

For most people, this is entirely unnecessary. It's possible to reap 80% of the rewards associated with good health with 20% of the effort.

That's what this section is about.

We're going to examine diet and fitness through the lens of the Pareto principle. You'll discover that achieving and maintaining good health requires neither complicated meal plans nor hours in the gym each day. I'll show you how to focus on the few factors that'll get you 80% of the way there.

A Quick Note Before We Proceed

It's worth repeating the purpose of this book. It's not my goal to advance your career, optimize your home life, improve your dating life, or help you to achieve your desired physique. Rather, my goal is to demonstrate the universal applicability of the 80/20 rule.

If you apply this rule to your career, your home life, your dating life, and your health, as well as to the areas we'll cover in Parts 5 through 7, you'll see amazing results. I guarantee it.

That's the nature of the 80/20 rule: to help you get more mileage from less effort in everything you do.

With that in mind, let's talk about how to use the 80/20 rule to live healthily without resorting to complicated diets and exercise routines.

EATING HEALTHY

~

Most of us can stand to eat healthier. Some of us occasionally indulge in our favorite treats. Others go on full-blown sugar benders. Still others eat emotionally; they're sad, stressed, or depressed, and use food for comfort.

All roads lead to the same destination. We end up gaining weight - albeit at different rates - and feeling guilty.

Many people react to this predicament by going on a hardcore diet. They vow to eschew all junk food, sticking exclusively to healthy foods. Depending on the diet, they load up on vegetables, fruits, fish, chicken, eggs, and various supplements.

For a few days, things go exactly as planned. The dieter

sticks to an ultra-strict meal regimen, forgoing anything that contains unhealthy ingredients.

But then the first signs of trouble appear. The dieter's willpower erodes to the point that it becomes impossible to resist the cravings for his or her favorite treats. Or the dieter has a terrible day at the office and grabs a sugary snack for comfort.

Before long, the diet has been abandoned, prompting feelings of guilt.

It doesn't have to be this way. The 80/20 rule shows us how to enjoy most of the benefits of eating healthily without taking draconian measures.

Maintain A Mostly-Clean Diet

Diet is a misnomer, at least in the context of eating for long-term health. The word implies a short-term pursuit. For example, we diet to lose weight, but plan to abandon the diet once we achieve our goal. We seldom admit this plan, but it's inherent in our undertaking.

So, let's shift our perspective. Rather than consider the merits of going on an extreme diet, let's talk about making small adjustments to our eating habits. In doing so, we'll achieve the majority of the benefits associated with healthy eating without the misery attendant to depriving ourselves completely of the foods we enjoy.

First, make a list of your favorite unhealthy foods. From potato chips and ice cream to donuts and pancakes. Don't hedge. Ice cream isn't healthy for the fact that it contains calcium.

Second, make a list of simple, healthy meals and snacks. The easier they are to prepare, the better.

Third, commit to sticking to these healthy meals and snacks 80% of the time. Give yourself permission to indulge 20% of the time. For example, suppose you have eggs for breakfast, a salmon fillet for lunch, and chicken and veggies for dinner. Allow yourself a small bowl of ice cream for dessert.

You don't need to deprive yourself completely to be healthy. In fact, doing so would likely do more harm than good. When it comes to food, moderation yields better long-term results than deprivation.

Avoid Dietary Traps At Restaurants

Many people who strive to eat healthily are averse to eating out. They figure they'll be unable to order foods that align with their goals. But this assumption is untrue. With a little planning, you can enjoy eating at most restaurants, confident that your meals are reasonably healthy.

First, don't be afraid to ask for changes on certain dishes. For example, if a dish comes with french fries, ask to replace them with veggies. If a dish sounds appealing, but comes with a lot of sauces, ask that the sauces be delivered on the side.

Second, ask for a take-home container when you place your order. When your dish arrives, place half of it in the container. This is a great way to apply portion control, important when you're dining in restaurants that serve dishes big enough for two people.

Third, if you and your dining partner plan to order the same meal, order one and split it. You'll probably find that it's enough to leave both of you feeling satisfied. In the unlikely event you're still hungry after splitting the meal, you can always order additional food.

These small adjustments will give you the freedom to eat out without fear of ruining your healthy eating habits. They take little effort, but offer a lot of flexibility.

Say No To Temptations At Social Affairs

Social engagements are tough on people who are trying to stick to eating healthy foods. Temptations lurk around every corner, and if healthy food is present, it's usually little more than window dressing. How can you stay on track when you're facing a cornucopia of foods that are bad for you?

The Pareto principle will help you to manage the temptations in a way that doesn't leave you feeling deprived. Whether you're attending a wedding, a friend's barbecue, or any other social event, rest assured you can enjoy yourself without betraying your nutritional goals.

First, eat something before you arrive at the event. Almonds and apples are good options because the contain fiber. The fiber will give you a sensation of satiety, which will prevent you from gorging later.

Second, allow 20% of the calories you eat to come from unhealthy foods. For example, if you're attending a friend's barbecue, eat chicken with a light coat of BBQ sauce. The chicken, arguably a healthy choice, will make up 80% of the meal's calories. The light coat of BBQ sauce will make up the other 20%.

Third, be willing to turn down food when it's offered to you. Don't feel as if you must accept a plate of artery-clogging snacks lest you hurt the host's feelings. You can turn it down in a way that's polite and respectful.

You don't need to stick to a 100% healthy diet to be healthy. The body is a wondrous machine that can metabolize a great variety of foods. Give yourself permission to indulge now and then.

You'll find that eating an 80% healthy diet is ten times easier than trying to maintain a *perfect* diet. And importantly, you'll still reap a majority of the benefits.

STAYING FIT

~

Physical activity is a vital part of any health plan. It not only aids in weight loss, but helps keep a variety of diseases at bay. The question is, how much exercise do you need to get to stay healthy? Is it necessary to spend hours a day pushing yourself to exhaustion? (You already know the answer.)

The fact is, there are smart tactics you can use to get into shape and stay fit while drastically slashing the time and effort you invest. As in previous sections, the 80/20 rule will be our guide.

Do Compound Exercises

One of the drawbacks of isolation exercises is that they take a lot of time. Each exercise targets a specific area of the body, which means a full-body workout requires going through a long list of movements. It can literally take hours.

Unless working out is your passion, you're probably averse to spending significant time doing it. The good news is, doing so is unnecessary. You can get into shape and stay fit with compound exercises. These are movements that target multiple joints and muscles. They save a lot of time while delivering multiple benefits (improved cardiovascular health, greater flexibility, and increased strength). This outcome defines the essence of the 80/20 rule.

First, identify your top priority. Are you trying to gain muscle mass? Lose fat? Get toned? Or are you mostly interested in increased stamina?

Second, pick compound exercises that support your top priority. For example, if your goal is to gain lower-body muscle mass, do barbell squats and barbell deadlifts. If you want to reduce fat, try plate twists, weighted bench dips, and walking lunges.

Third, create a *short* workout routine based on these compound exercises. I'm an advocate of making slow, incremental progress. That being the case, I recommend limiting your workout to 10 minutes a day for the first two weeks. Don't over do it. Focus on building the habit. You can extend the duration of your workout later.

The great thing about compound exercises is that they do more than just save time compared to isolation exercises. They also burn more calories, build coordination, and improve muscle efficiency.

In other words, big results with less action: the 80/20 rule in practice.

Focus On One Major Fitness Goal

We touched on this subject above, but it's worth mentioning in its own right.

There are many types of fitness goals. For example, you might want to gain muscle mass, lose weight, reduce your BMI, increase your endurance, or build your strength. While all of these may sound appealing, it's helpful to focus on the one or two that are most important to you.

Pursuing these top-priority goals will inevitably yield improvements across the board. For example, if you do exercises designed to build muscle mass, you'll likely reduce your BMI in the process. If you do exercises designed to help you shed weight, you'll probably build greater endurance along the way.

Such results are the bedrock of the Pareto principle. Here's the approach I recommend:

First, write down your goals and rate them according to importance. This is merely a snapshot of where you are today. If you're carrying a few extra pounds, losing weight might be your *current* priority, and thus rate higher than building muscle mass. Two months from now, after you've dropped the extra pounds, you can revisit your goals and rerank them.

Second, turn your top-priority goal into a S.M.A.R.T. goal. This acronym stands for specific (S), measurable (M), attainable (A), relevant (R), and time-based (T). A S.M.A.R.T. goal related to weight loss might look like the following: *to experience more energy, I'll lose two pounds a week over the course of eight weeks via daily exercises performed at home.*

Third, obtain a daily calendar that displays the next eight weeks. Use it to monitor your workout activity. Each day, after you finish your exercises, cross the day off on your calendar. Use a red pen. When you see an unbroken string of red X's, you'll be disinclined to break your streak.

The 80/20 Rule Of Fitness

Although the 80/20 rule can be observed in every facet of our lives, nowhere is it so evident than in the arena of fitness. You can literally get into shape with 15 to 20 minutes of exercise each day.

And it doesn't have to be grueling exercise. I do pushups and take short walks. If I'm watching something on Netflix, I may do a few squats. That's it. I'm reasonably healthy and tend to have plenty of energy.

Bottom line: regular physical activity is important. But the fact is, our bodies don't need a ton of it to stay fit. When the *right* exercises (based on our fitness goals) are combined with a healthy eating plan, a little goes a long way.

SAVING TIME

~

As I mentioned earlier, all of us are busy. Time is one of our most precious resources simply because it's so limited. And once it's gone, it's gone forever.

So getting maximum results from our diet and fitness regimen with the least amount of time invested is a major advantage. The time we save is time we can use toward other interests and pursuits.

That's the reason we're focusing so closely on the 80/20 rule. That's why we're allowing it to guide our decisions. When it comes to diet and exercise, there's no reason to spend more time than necessary toward achieving our goals. Life's too short.

With that in mind, here are a few ways to ensure you're producing maximum results with minimum inputs.

Exercise At Home

There are advantages to working out in a gym. Gyms offer expensive equipment, you can easily find spotters, and there's an atmosphere that encourages you to push yourself.

But visiting a gym every time you want to work out also takes a lot of time. Not only should you take into account the commute to the gym, but you might be forced to wait for the equipment you want to use. Worse, gyms can be distracting as you may have to listen to people grunting or screaming.

I strongly recommend exercising at home. You'll be better able to focus in your own personal space. That, in addition to not having to wait for equipment, will help you to finish your workouts more quickly. (And keep in mind, there's no commute.) Here's how to start:

First, review the exercises you listed in the previous section. These are the compound exercises that complement your top-priority fitness goal.

Second, determine the equipment you'll need to perform these exercises. You may be able to get by with little more than an adjustable bench and bar, a few dumbbells, some bands for resistance training, and an exercise mat. Think bare bones. There's no need to load up on equipment if you don't need it.

Third, designate a separate room - perhaps your garage - as your home gym. You'll want to be able to close the door and focus.

One of the great things about exercising at home is that the gym is open 24 hours a day and 365 days a year. You can visit whenever you desire. As a bonus, you can do it without having to pay membership fees.

Focus On Exercises That Matter

Fitness programs often suffer from "exercise creep." An individual hears that certain movements are beneficial and adds them to his or her workout routine. Or perhaps he or she does so to inject variety into the workout. Either way, one by one, these extra movements steadily increase the time needed to complete the exercise session.

While these additional exercises may prove beneficial, it's likely they're inconsistent with the individual's top-priority goal. At the very least, they're probably unnecessary, needlessly duplicating the individual's efforts and wasting his or her time.

Here again, the Pareto principle is a terrific tool for cutting out the nonessential and focusing on what matters.

First, remind yourself that 80% of your forward progress will stem from a minority of exercises. Another way to think of this is that you don't need to do *more* exercises. You just need to do the *right* ones.

Second, realize that variety doesn't matter in the context of working out. Your muscles and joints will not adapt to specific movements and develop a tolerance against them. As long as you've chosen the appropriate compound exercises given your fitness goals, you can confidently stick with them. Don't replace them for variety's sake.

Third, avoid "exercise creep" at all costs. Before adding a new movement to your fitness routine, ask yourself why it's necessary. The fact that the movement is beneficial is not a good enough reason to incorporate it.

Focusing on the right exercises will save you significant time while delivering the majority of the fitness benefits you're seeking. Yes, you can spend a lot of time perfecting your routine to squeeze additional mileage from it. But getting 80% of the way there while spending minimal time and effort is, in my opinion, a preferable strategy.

Experiment With High-Intensity Interval Training (HIIT)

High-intensity interval training can be one of the purest applications of the Pareto principle when it comes to fitness. It focuses on intense bursts of effort over short periods.

An example is to sprint for 30 seconds followed by a 4-minute rest. This short rest period is followed by another 30-second sprint. Another example is to do 10 rapid-fire pushups followed by a 20-second rest. After resting for 20 second, you'd do 10 more pushups.

The upside of this intense approach is that you work harder in an abbreviated time frame, take in more oxygen, and burn more calories and fat. The results are often remarkable. If you've ever seen someone with an ultra-toned physique, it's likely he or she practices HIIT.

This practice aligns nicely with the 80/20 rule. HIIT consumes very little time compared to conventional work-outs, yet delivers astounding results. For this reason, I encourage you to experiment with it.

First, start with Tabata training. It involves 20 seconds of high-intensity exercise followed by 10 seconds of rest. You're expected to complete eight reps. The type of exercise is up to you. Pushups, squats, lunges, jumping jacks, etc. all qualify.

Second, start with a single HIIT session per week. Because of its intensity, it's easy to overdo it. After a few weeks of performing this type of training, start doing two weekly sessions. After a few more weeks have passed, increase it to three.

Third, take the time to warm up. It's possible to injure yourself if you jump into HIIT without first priming your joints and muscles for action.

HIIT is an excellent fitness strategy because you don't have to set aside an hour to enjoy a full workout. Eight repetitions, each comprised of 20 seconds of intense exercise followed by 10 seconds of rest, takes four minutes.

Experiment with it. You stand to reap big benefits without investing a lot of time. That, of course, cuts to the heart of the 80/20 rule.

PART V

HOW TO 80/20 YOUR FINANCES

～

Many people are intimidated by money matters. They're daunted by all things related to budgeting, investing, retirement planning, and credit management.

One of the reasons is that they're confronted by a myriad of options. Having so many choices leads to confusion, which hampers their ability to make confident decisions.

It doesn't help that financial institutions regularly introduce new financial products, some with labyrinthine rules and regulations. It's difficult to know which products are beneficial and which are more likely to benefit the companies promoting them.

But imagine if you were able to manage all of your money-related needs, from budgeting to investing, spending just a few minutes each month. Moreover, suppose you were able to confidently make decisions, completely sidestepping the bewildering chaos of choosing from an endless array of financial products.

In this section, I'll show you how to 80/20 your financial life. We'll use the Pareto principle to simplify money matters so you'll never again feel intimidated by them.

Let's start with budgeting.

USE THE PARETO PRINCIPLE TO STREAMLINE YOUR BUDGET

~

I f you review your monthly bills, you'll see evidence of the 80/20 rule in action. For example, 80% of your grocery bill probably stems from 20% of the products you purchase. In fact, 80% of the money you spend each month probably goes toward 20% of the items you spend it on.

That's helpful to know because it simplifies budgeting. Once you identify the items that take up most of your budget, you can determine which of those expenditures are necessary and which are not. You can then easily create a budget that gives you a firm grip on your finances.

Let's start by figuring out where your money goes each month.

Track Your Fixed And Variable Expenses

Fixed expenses are those for which you pay the same amount each month. This constant makes them easy to fit into a budget. An example of a fixed expense is your car payment. Other examples include your mortgage payment, car insurance premiums, gym membership fee, and whatever you pay for internet service.

Variable expenses are those with amounts that vary each month. Examples include your grocery bill, clothing expenditures, and the money you spend on entertainment.

First, make a list of your routine monthly expenditures - both fixed and variable.

Second, mark the ones that are necessary. We need to distinguish them from your discretionary spending.

Third, add up the necessary expenditures.

Tallying variable expenses takes more time than tallying fixed expenses. But it's relatively simple. Review the amount of money you spent on each variable expense over the last three months. Then, divide the amounts by three to calculate a monthly average for each one.

This process is simpler if you use a credit card as you can just refer to your monthly statements. If you typically pay with cash, you'll need to refer to your receipts.

Either way, we now have a baseline of your necessary expenses. The total represents your monthly "nut." It's the amount you must spend each month to keep your head above water.

Track Your Discretionary Spending

Discretionary expenses are, by definition, unnecessary. They're the expenditures you can cut from your budget if you were in dire financial straits.

You may consider some discretionary expenses as necessary simply because they've become a part of your lifestyle. For example, you might think that life would be dismal without your Netflix subscription. Or you may argue that your daily coffee and croissant from Starbucks are imperative to your morning productivity.

In truth, you can get by without them if you were forced to do so.

It's important to make that distinction to clarify your monthly spending habits. That's the only way to ensure your budget is factual, and thereby a reliable tool.

First, make a list of your discretionary expenditures. Include big items you've purchased in the last six months, such as new cell phones, gaming consoles, or golf clubs.

Second, determine the average amount you spend on these items each month. Some will be easy to calculate. For example, if you spend $7 a day, five days a week, on a coffee and croissant from Starbucks, your monthly average is $140. For big purchases, estimate the amount you spend each year and divide the number by twelve. For example, suppose you spend $600 to buy a new cell phone each year. If so, your monthly average for this item would by $50.

Third, tally the monthly total.

This list of monthly discretionary expenditures is valuable. It gives you flexibility. If you need to cut things from your budget to save money, this is where to start cutting.

This list also provides clarity. It's difficult to know where our money goes - and why it goes so quickly - each month unless we track the individual expenditures. Doing so eliminates the uncertainty, and provides useful, actionable information in the process.

Saving Money For Big Expenditures

We now have the information we need to create a simple budget. We're aware of our necessary expenditures and recognize how much we spend on discretionary purchases.

But we should add a third element to our budget: how much to save each month for large, planned expenditures. That way, we can avoid borrowing money to fund them, and needlessly paying interest on that money.

For example, suppose you'd like to visit New York City with your spouse. You estimate the trip will cost $6,000. If you plan to go in 12 months, you'll need to save $500 per month to pay for the trip.

It's important to add these types of big expenditures to your monthly budget. The alternative is to pay them with your credit card without having the funds to cover the balance at the end of the month. This would force you to pay interest on the amount, which would unnecessarily - and perhaps drastically - increase the size of the total outlay.

First, make a list of every large purchase you intend to make over the next 12 months.

Second, calculate a monthly average for each one based on the amount and when you plan to make the purchase.

Third, add this monthly average to your budget.

Creating a household budget doesn't have to be complicated. Most of your income probably goes toward a small number of monthly expenses, some fixed and some variable, some necessary and some discretionary.

That's the 80/20 rule in action. All you have to do is identify these expenses, and determine how much you spend on each of them. Then, it becomes a simple matter of making adjustments to accommodate your needs.

By the way, I strongly recommend that you put your budget into a spreadsheet. That'll allow you to adjust the numbers and immediately see how the changes affect your monthly total. (I like using Google Sheets because it's simple, free, and in the cloud, where I can access it on my phone.)

OPTIMIZE YOUR
INVESTMENT/RETIREMENT PORTFOLIO

∿

I f there's one area related to money that causes people to hyperventilate, it's investing. There's a dizzying range of options, and even the simplest among them can seem complex.

Worse, the language that accompanies investing can seem downright foreign. Terms such as dividend yield, capital gains reinvestment, and price-to-earnings (P/E) ratio can be baffling to the uninitiated. And then there are different share classes to consider, as well as details regarding tax-exempt income, value versus growth investing, and dollar-cost averaging.

Mutual funds are supposed to make things easier. But there are different types from which to choose. Should you invest in a hedge fund, equity fund, or bond fund? If the latter, should you put your money into a fund composed mainly of government bonds, investment-grade corporate bonds, or high-yield bonds?

It's no wonder so many people avoid the subject. It seems to require a specialized degree just to understand what's going on.

But I have good news. You *can* be a successful investor without spending your evenings and weekends learning the trade. The key is to apply the 80/20 rule. Using it as your guide, you'll find that investing can be simple, easy, and require very little time while adding to your wealth.

A quick disclaimer: none of what follows should be considered investment advice.

Analyzing Stocks

When you think of stock investing, you might imagine someone sitting at his or her desk, closely watching several monitors. This individual buys and sells shares, often making split-second decisions, when the numbers and graphs on the monitors behave in a certain way.

Or maybe you picture someone scrutinizing reams of charts and other data, all in the hopes of finding that single promising stock that's worth buying. This individual spends hours doing research before making a decision.

Investing in stocks doesn't have to be this complicated. Nor should it take so much time and effort. The truth is, you can analyze a stock in minutes by focusing on the few numbers that matter most and ignoring the rest.

First, note the stock's P/E ratio. Compare it to the P/E ratios of its competitors. Lower is better.

Second, calculate the company's return on equity (ROE). That may sound daunting, but it's actually simple. All you have to do is divide the company's net income by its shareholders equity. Net income can be found on the company's income statement. Shareholders equity can be found on the company's balance sheet.

Third, calculate the company's price/earnings growth (PEG) ratio. Again, this sounds complicated, but it's easy. All you have to do is divide the P/E ratio by the company's earnings growth rate (EPS). EPS figures can be found online at places like Nasdaq.com. PEG ratios under 1 are favorable.

These three numbers - P/E ratio, ROE, and PEG ratio - provide the information you need to decide whether you should buy a particular stock. Yes, you can do a *lot* more analysis. But the time and effort involved is unlikely to have a major impact. Stick to these three figures and ignore the rest.

Incidentally, I advocate a buy-and-hold strategy when it comes to stocks. It simplifies investing and is more effective than trying to time the market. And the best part? It takes a lot less time.

Are Mutual Funds The Answer?

I'm a big believer in mutual funds. For context, I have a college degree in investments and securities. Much of the curriculum focused on analyzing stocks and picking winners. Yet today, I invest most of my money in mutual funds.

The reason is simple: the 80/20 rule.

Over the last 30+ years, I've discovered that mutual funds, when chosen properly, can produce an annual return that rivals that from picking stocks. And it takes a fraction of the time and effort - literally less than 60 seconds a month.

Following is the approach I use to invest in mutual funds. (Again, this is not to be taken as investment advice.)

First, I visit Vanguard.com. I like Vanguard because they offer no-load funds (no commission or sales charge) and low expense ratios.

Second, I pick several index funds and compare them side by side. I focus on their respective expense ratios, portfolios (I prefer domestic stocks and bonds), and the growth of $10,000 placed into the funds 10 years prior. This latter detail is displayed in helpful graphs on the Vanguard website.

Third, I select the best fund from the litter.

That's it. I put money into the fund once a month. And because the Vanguard site is so intuitive, I can do it in less than 60 seconds. Meanwhile, I know my money is being expertly managed by a team that has a decades-long track record.

Investing In Real Estate

A lot of people enjoy investing in real estate. Some buy residential properties, fix them up, and flip them for a profit. Others buy properties and rent them to tenants, generating monthly cashflow.

Both are fine ways to reap the rewards of real estate investing. But they take a lot of time and effort. For example, buying and flipping properties requires getting them into good enough shape that they're appealing to buyers. Owning rental properties means becoming a de facto landlord, which present its own challenges.

There's an easier way to invest in real estate: buy shares in real estate investment trusts, or REITs. Doing so delegates the hassles associated with buying and flipping or being a landlord.

The beauty of REITs is their simplicity. You benefit financially from the appreciation and rental income generated by the properties held in the trust. At the same time, you avoid the inconveniences that come with conventional real estate investments.

It's a great example of the Pareto principle in action.

If I were to invest in REITs, I'd follow similar steps to the ones described regarding investing in mutual funds.

First, I'd visit Vanguard.com.

Second, I'd compare select details between several relevant funds offered by Vanguard. This includes Vanguard's flagship REIT as well as index funds that invest in REITs offered by other companies.

Third, I'd pick one or two, and put money into them each month.

Investing only *seems* complicated, and only if you've never done it. In reality, it's simple. Apply the 80/20 rule to your investment decisions, focusing on the few important details and ignoring everything else. If you do so, you can build a promising portfolio while spending minimal time.

APPLY THE 80/20 RULE TO YOUR CREDIT CARDS

~

C redit cards are a wonderful tool if they're used properly. At the same time, if they're misman-aged, they can become the bane of one's existence.

You probably know someone who went deep into debt and struggled to climb his or her way out. Perhaps you've experienced the nightmare of suffocating under a mountain of credit card debt yourself.

I've met people who proudly display dozens of cards, and frankly I've been baffled. I always imagine the cards are more trouble than they're worth. The more cards you have to manage, the more likely something will escape notice and cause problems later.

I encourage you to apply the 80/20 rule to your credit

cards. Streamline how you use them, and you'll be less likely to miss something important. And if you play your cards right, you'll benefit by obtaining rewards that are relevant to you (more on this below).

Get Rid Of Unnecessary Credit Cards

You can get by with just one or two credit cards. Additional cards are unnecessary.

Having more cards won't help your credit score. Two cards are arguably better for your score than 10 assuming the two cards aren't maxed out. (Credit bureaus take utilization rate into account.)

Nor will having more cards give you more financial flexibility. Possessing two cards, each boasting a large credit line, is the same as possessing 10 cards, each with a small credit line. If anything, keeping more cards will burden you with more fees.

Lastly, obtaining several cards for the rewards is unlikely to help you in the long run. You'll end up spending a lot of time trying to maximize rewards that fail to pay off.

A few years ago, I applied for a Discover card. I had never had one (nor had use for one), but kept hearing good things about the card. So I requested one. And never used it.

A year later, Discover sent me a letter. They essentially said, "Use the card in 30 days or we're going to yank your account." So I used it.

The thing is, using it was a terrible idea. I don't need

the Discover card. It sits in a drawer gathering dust. That being the case, the next time Discover threatens to pull my account, I'm going to let them. It's one less thing for me to think about.

If you have a lot of credit cards, I recommend that you get rid of all but two of them. Two is plenty.

First, list your cards along with their respective credit lines and interest rates.

Second, pick two cards. Ideally, these cards will be the ones that offer the largest credit lines, lowest interest rates, and best rewards.

Third, call the companies that issued the other cards and ask them to close the accounts. Make sure you pay the balances beforehand.

These days, there's no reason to maintain several cards. Use the 80/20 rule. Put the majority of your purchases on a single card. Keep a second card for emergencies. Discard the rest.

Fewer cards means fewer headaches.

Focus On Rewards That Are Important To You

If you're maintaining certain credit cards to take advantage of the rewards, make sure the rewards are relevant to you. For example, suppose you have a credit card solely for the travel-related rewards. But you don't travel enough to take advantage of it. In that case, why keep it?

Also, make sure your desired rewards aren't duplicated by other cards. For example, suppose you have three cards that give you cash back for purchases made with them. Further suppose the cash-back percentage is the same across all three accounts. If you only use one of the cards, why keep the other two? You're not going to take advantage of their cards' cash-back feature.

Use the Pareto principle to decide which rewards-based cards to keep (or apply for) and which to get rid of. Here's how:

First, identify the two rewards that most interest you. For example, if you travel a lot, you might be particularly interested in airline miles and hotel points. If you drive a lot, you might want a card that offers gas rewards. If you buy everything with a credit card, a cash-back reward makes sense.

Second, close accounts associated with any cards that don't offer these two rewards. Also, close accounts associated with any cards that *duplicate* these rewards.

Third, use your reward card whenever possible. Use it at restaurants, grocery stores, at Amazon.com, and hotels. If you have recurring payments set up - for example, your gym membership or Netflix account - have them charged to your reward card. Charge *everything*. That'll help you to accrue the rewards as quickly as possible.

Consolidate Multiple Credit Card Balances

Ideally, you'd pay off your credit card balances at the end of each month. That way, you can avoid paying interest charges.

But paying off balances before the interest starts to accrue is not always possible. Emergencies can cause your balances to balloon, and leave you struggling to manage them. And the more balances you have, the more difficult they are to manage.

If you have balances on multiple cards, use the 80/20 rule as a guide for simplifying things. Apply for a single balance transfer card that you can use to consolidate your accounts. Then, once the accounts have been consolidated, focus on paying down that one resulting balance.

First, apply for a balance transfer card that offers a reasonably low interest rate and a low transfer fee. The best cards of this sort refrain from charging a transfer fee while offering a 0% introductory APR.

Second, transfer as many of your cards as possible to this new account.

Third, close all but one of the old accounts after the transfers have been completed. Keep that account open for emergencies.

After completing the transfers, you'll have a single due date to remember and a single balance to pay down. This is much easier to manage than juggling several cards.

Simpler is always better when it comes to using credit cards. I strongly encourage you to keep the Pareto principle in mind. You can get just as much bang for your buck using one or two carefully-selected rewards cards as you can trying to manage several accounts at once.

PART VI

HOW TO 80/20 YOUR EDUCATION AND TRAINING

~

You're going to learn new things throughout your life. Whether that happens as a result of reading books, performing your job, or watching TED talks, your brain will immediately try to store the information.

For some people, learning new things is its own reward. The discovery of new concepts and ideas, or the mastery of new skills, is, by itself, reason to celebrate.

For others, learning stems from *purpose*. These individuals learn to accomplish a specific goal. It's a step toward advancing their careers, earning more money, increasing their productivity, or boosting their value to others.

I'm in the second group. When I set out to learn something, I do so for a specific purpose. I try to learn things quickly because I want to apply the new knowledge or skill in the present to achieve a particular outcome.

This section is written from that perspective. I'm going to show you how to use the Pareto principle to learn and apply new material in a way that delivers maximum results. Moreover, our goal is to do so in as short a time frame as possible.

MAKE THE MOST OF YOUR LEARNING TIME

~

P eople learn in different ways. The effectiveness of these different strategies varies from person to person.

Having said that, there are several universal truths regarding how the brain absorbs new information and commits it to memory. If you acknowledge these truths and pursue new material in a manner that accommodates them, you can expedite the learning process and improve your retention.

Below, in accordance with the 80/20 rule, we'll focus on the tactics that have the greatest effect. There are dozens of tactics you can use to improve your learning. But we're going to concentrate on those that'll move the needle furthest with respect to getting things done and realizing your goals.

Let's start by examining *where* you choose to learn.

Choose A Distraction-Free Learning Space

Most people struggle with concentration. They can focus for a few minutes at a time, but become distracted during longer periods. This is problematic when they attempt to learn new material or master new skills. The process takes longer than necessary. Worse, retention suffers.

If you find it difficult to focus, there's a simple solution: find a distraction-free study environment.

First, consider your options. Perhaps you can study in your bedroom, closing the door to discourage interruptions. Or maybe you'd be better served visiting your local public or campus library. Perhaps your local coffeeshop offers a quiet ambiance.

Second, sever all electronic links to the outside world while you study. Turn off your phone; avoid checking your email; and ignore Facebook, Instagram, and Twitter.

Third, if you decide to study in a location that attracts other people (e.g. a coffeehouse, public library, etc.), bring headphones. That way, you can listen to music. The music will drown out the ambient noise in the environment. As a bonus, the headphones will discourage people from interrupting you.

There are many things you can do to improve your ability to learn. But this single tactic - i.e. choosing a distraction-free environment - will have the greatest impact in terms of helping your brain process new information.

Use Time Chunks For Concentrated Study Sessions

It's tempting to power through long study sessions. After all, you want to maintain your momentum and avoid wasting time. But in truth, taking breaks is beneficial to your learning. Your brain needs frequent downtime to process new information and commit it to memory.

If you study without taking breaks, your focus and retention will inevitably erode. Worse, the rate of erosion will increase as time passes. Eventually, the time you spend studying will be wasted as your brain becomes unable to store the material for future retrieval.

As above, there are many ways to tackle this problem. But we're following the Pareto principle, which means we want to identify the tactic that'll have the greatest effect. To that end, I strongly encourage you to organize your study sessions into time chunks.

First, decide in advance how long you'll study before taking a break. I recommend studying in 30-minute chunks, each of which is followed by a 5-minute break. Having said that, I encourage you to experiment. You might find that you're able to focus for 60 minutes, and can make better use of 15-minute breaks between sessions. There are no hard and fast rules when it comes to using time chunks. A word of advice: use a timer to remind yourself when to take breaks so you don't have to keep looking at a clock.

Second, make a list of things you'll do during your breaks. Focus on activities that allow you to unplug. For example, rather than checking Facebook, take a walk outside, fix a healthy snack, or phone a friend for a brief chat. These activities will give your brain the time it needs to replenish its attentional resources.

Third, create a study plan. Rather than approaching new material haphazardly, set a schedule that details what you'll focus on during each time chunk. Doing so will keep you organized and moving forward. For example, you might divide a 50-minute time chunk into two parts: 40 minutes to study your chosen topic and 10 minutes to test your mastery of it.

Study The Material That'll Have The Greatest Influence

This tactic is *pure* 80/20.

The biggest challenge you're likely to face when learning new material is that you'll have limited time to do so. If you're a student, you're responsible for completing assignments and projects, and preparing for exams - usually for several classes. If you're an executive, you're responsible for tasks, projects, and meetings that take up the majority of your day. If you're a stay-at-home parent, you're responsible for an endless list of tasks and errands.

So carving out time to learn new things is easier said than done.

For this reason, it's critical that you focus on learning the most important stuff, and avoid wasting time on nonessential details. For example, suppose you want to learn how to use Photoshop. You'd be best served focusing your time on mastering the features you'll use most often (e.g. layers, built-in presets, spot healing brush, etc.).

How do you know what you should focus on? I recommend you take the following steps.

First, start with your purpose. Ask yourself why you're learning the new material. How do you intend to use your newfound knowledge or newly-developed skill? In other words, what is your desired outcome?

Second, identify the aspects of your subject matter that'll help you the most in accomplishing what you'd like to achieve. For example, suppose you'd like to learn to play the guitar. If you're mainly interested in playing simple songs, you'd do well to focus on chord construction. On the other hand, if you'd like to play like Eddie Van Halen, you should focus on scales, modes, and dexterity exercises.

Third, ignore the rest.

There's simply no time to learn every detail about your chosen topic. You have other responsibilities. Given that fact, it's advisable to learn new things and develop new faculties as quickly as possible.

Trust the 80/20 rule. Focus on the material and exercises that promise to deliver the biggest results within the shortest time frame.

COMPLETE ASSIGNMENTS, PROJECTS, AND TASKS MORE QUICKLY

~

As I implied in the introduction to this section, we're not striving for perfection. Rather, we're learning new material and developing new skills for specific purposes.

The Pareto principle does not abide perfectionism. On the contrary, it encourages the individual to get 80% of the way to his or her objective while expending only 20% of the available resources to do so. It notes that the law of diminishing returns takes hold at that point. Each additional unit of time and effort generates a steadily-decreasing return.

This concept gives us the freedom and impetus to learn things quickly. Once we're willing to abandon perfectionism in the context of our education and training, we can devote our attention to learning for the purpose of generating results.

This application of the 80/20 rule will allow you to get things done faster. And importantly, you'll know that you're leveraging your limited time, allocating it toward its most efficient and productive use.

Recognize That Doing A Perfect Job Is A Short-Lived Success

Suppose you're a student and receive a perfect score on your latest assignment. How large an impact will that score have on your academic career?

Suppose you're a project manager and complete your latest project with zero errors. You may receive accolades in the present, but will anybody care next month?

Suppose you're a photographer and produce a technically perfect photograph. How long do you expect to be praised for your meticulousness?

The point is, doing a perfect job seldom, if ever, generates long-term benefits. Such successes are short-lived. That's an important point to consider. If our goal in learning things is to satisfy specific purposes, there's limited value in using our newfound knowledge and skills to do a perfect job. Doing so is contrary to our aim.

Applying new knowledge and skills plays a crucial role in the learning process. But it's important to recognize the counterproductive nature of trying to do things perfectly.

Depending on your habits and history, this might require a small shift in perspective.

First, acknowledge that perfectionism is an unhealthy compulsion.

Second, accept that time spent using your newfound knowledge or newly-developed skills to do a perfect job is time *wasted*.

Third, remind yourself that your ultimate goal in learning new things is to become more effective, more productive, and ultimately more valuable. Perfectionism has nothing to do with these outcomes.

Focus Your Time And Attention On High-Impact Tasks

With respect to increasing your productivity, your goal should never be to get everything done. Instead, your goal should be to get the most *important* things done.

To that end, whenever you broaden your knowledge or expand your skillset, you should focus on applications that produce the biggest results. That's how you can take fullest advantage of whatever new concept or ability you've learned.

That's the 80/20 rule in a nutshell: doing more with less.

The problem is, it's often difficult to know how to take action on new knowledge and skills so they'll yield the greatest impact. Following is a simple plan for doing so.

First, write down your purpose for learning the new

information or skill. It's useful to have this purpose in writing in front of you. It'll keep you focused.

Second, make a list of the tasks you can now tackle thanks to your newly-developed expertise.

Third, observe each task on your list through the lens of your purpose. Rank each one according to its anticipated effect.

These three simple steps will clarify where you should spend your time and attention. They'll highlight the few tasks that'll produce the biggest results, allowing you to take maximum advantage of whatever you've learned.

Accept Less-Than-Perfect Results As The Cost Of Efficiency

It's more important to be efficient than perfect. Being efficient means you're getting things done in a methodical manner. Moreover, you're doing so in a way that makes the best use of your resources.

Have you ever known someone who has a busy schedule, and thus little time to waste, yet manages to be extremely productive? This individual probably gets more *important* work done than people who have twice the amount of time at their disposal.

He or she is ultra-efficient. I can guarantee this person isn't obsessed with producing perfect results. *Imperfect* results are the accepted cost of sustained efficiency.

When you develop a new expertise, it's natural to want to use it to do the best possible job. Perfect results serve as validation that you've improved yourself in a measurable way. But again, for our purposes, it's more important to be efficient than perfect. The question is, how do you find the right balance?

First, remind yourself of your purpose in pursuing new training and education. What are you trying to accomplish?

Second, identify your desired outcome. This will be an extension of your purpose. For example, suppose you're learning how to create pivot tables in your favorite spreadsheet program. Let's say you're doing so to be able to do your job better. That's your *purpose*. Your *desired outcome* is to acquire the ability to organize data within your spreadsheet so you can extract maximum insight from them.

Third, acknowledge that you don't need to become an expert at pivot tables to achieve your purpose and produce your desire outcome. You just need to learn how to use them well enough to be efficient.

Again, we learn things to effect forward progress. Since you're reading this book, it's safe to assume you do it to become more effective, more productive, and more valuable. Give yourself the freedom to abandon perfection in the name of getting more done. You'll be able to leverage your time and effort and take quicker advantage of your new expertise.

ADJUST YOUR ATTITUDE CONCERNING SUCCESS AND FAILURE

∼

Many people consider success and failure to comprise an either-or scenario. You either succeed or you fail. There's no middle ground.

Moreover, they apply strict parameters to failure so they can easily identify it. For example, a student might consider any score below an "A" to be a failure. An executive may consider any delay in the project he or she is spearheading to constitute failure. A stay-at-home parent might believe his or her child's tantrum signifies failure on his or her part.

This mindset does more harm than good. It suggests that failure is absolute and worthy of criticism. Worse, it encourages the individual to feel as if they should give up.

In truth, all outcomes, both positive or negative, are learning opportunities. Negative outcomes don't imply failure as much as suggest the value of revisiting objectives and considering different, and hopefully more effective, approaches. Moreover, *positive* outcomes signal that we're on the right track, even if our results fail to meet perfectionistic standards.

Whenever we apply new knowledge or skills, we should focus on improvements in our productivity. We may not produce perfect results. We may not even effect *positive* results. But that doesn't matter. Our new expertise, whether it's a firmer grasp of vital information or increased proficiency in a new skill, still improves our effectiveness.

And that makes us more productive in the long run.

Cultivate A Growth Mindset

The idea of a growth mindset was popularized by Dr. Carol Dweck in her book *Mindset: The New Psychology Of Success*. In short, people who have this mindset believe they can develop practically any skill through hard work and persistence. By contrast, people who have a fixed mindset believe that success stems from talent. You're either born with that talent or you're not.

A growth mindset is essential if you want to take full advantage of the Pareto principle. The principle itself is grounded in the fact that improvement is perpetual. If we focus on the small number of inputs that continually produce the biggest results, we can engineer success in any endeavor we pursue.

So, how do you develop a growth mindset?

First, look for opportunities to learn new skills and concepts that align with your goals. Recall our earlier example where you'd like to learn how to create pivot tables within spreadsheets to be more effective at your job. Look for video tutorials that teach the subject on Youtube. Or take an online class that teaches pivot tables in a business-related context.

Second, be willing to meet challenges head-on. Learning new material and putting it to productive use is sometimes difficult. You're bound to confront roadblocks. Face such challenges directly and you'll become more resilient to them in the future.

Third, maintain your sense of purpose. If you can articulate your reason for developing an expertise, you'll be more likely to accomplish the goal you've set for yourself.

Cultivating a growth mindset gives you the confidence to learn new ideas and develop new skills. All you have to do is apply yourself whenever the need arises. Meanwhile, maintaining your sense of purpose guides your efforts, ensuring they complement your agenda.

Embrace Constructive Criticism

It's natural to feel defensive when someone criticizes us. Criticism feels like an accusation of failure. Ergo, we immediately feel as if our competence is under attack.

But in truth, constructive criticism can be a powerful tool, particularly if it's offered by someone we respect. It need not be a charge of failure. Instead, it can pave the road toward personal growth, helping us to resolve issues that hamper our effectiveness.

I've found that being open to criticism allows me to get more mileage out of everything I learn. If I apply a new skill poorly, I can count on constructive advice from my network to help me improve. If my grasp of a new concept is faulty, I can rely on feedback from friends and acquaintances to enhance my understanding.

Such constructive criticism has proven to be vital to my growth in every aspect of my life. So I encourage you to learn to embrace it yourself. Here's how:

First, recognize that people don't offer constructive advice to make you feel bad. They do so in the hopes that you'll benefit from it. So there's no need to feel defensive.

Second, ask the person offering the feedback to give you specifics. It's one thing for a friend to say, "Your guitar playing needs a little polish." It's much more helpful if your friend points out that your chords sound muddy, you're playing too fast, and you're strumming too hard.

Third, take action on the advice. For example, practice forming clear-sounding chords, playing more slowly, and strumming more softly. The more you act on the (good) advice you're given, the more you'll see future feedback as an opportunity to improve.

I encourage you to harness the new things you learn throughout your life by applying the 80/20 rule. You don't need to become an expert on anything. Nor do you need to produce flawless results with your newfound expertise. Rather, start with a purpose, and then concentrate on the few inputs related to your training that promise to generate the majority of your results.

You'll enjoy the learning process more, and you'll see fast evidence that you're becoming more effective.

PART VII

HOW TO 80/20 YOUR SMALL BUSINESS

~

If you run a small business, even if it's just a side gig, you know from experience how much time and work are involved with keeping it on track. And if you're running the business while working full-time, you know how crazily hectic it can become as the workload increases in both areas of your life.

But what if you could grow your business while making your life easier in the process? What if you had a way to expand your customer base and multiply your revenue without working 70+ hours a week?

The Pareto principle can help you to do precisely that. It'll show you where to spend your time, effort, and capital for maximum effect. It'll also highlight areas in which you're leaving money on the table.

As you know, the core idea behind the 80/20 rule is to get more done with less effort. Nowhere is that more important than in running a small business. As the owner, you'll be wearing a lot of hats, particularly when you start out. Knowing which hats are important and which are trivial can save you a massive amount of time while catapulting your revenue.

If you adhere to the 80/20 rule as your business grows, you'll be astounded by your momentum.

MAXIMIZE YOUR SALES AND MARKETING EFFORTS

~

Sales and marketing are integral to running a business. Success largely stems from discoverability and continued visibility (good products and solid customer service are givens). You need to bring new prospects into your orbit. You also need to encourage your current customers to buy more.

In order to do these things, you must get and stay in front of your audience. That's the purpose of sales and marketing.

The good news is, there are hundreds of things you can do to get the word out about your business. The bad news is, most of these things are ineffective. They'll do little more than suck up your limited time and capital.

Here's where the 80/20 rule can be your most

powerful ally. If you can identify the 20% of the tactics that bring in 80% of your revenue, you can achieve rapid growth. Moreover, you can do so without needlessly spinning your wheels on ineffective sales and marketing ideas.

With that in mind, let's take a look at one of your most important assets: your existing customers.

Identify Your Best Customers

Business owners tend to treat their customers equally. They give each customer the same level of service and expect each customer to comply with the same set of rules.

In my opinion, this is a misguided practice.

According to the Pareto principle, 20% of your customers will generate 80% of your sales. Moreover, 20% of your customers will generate 80% of your customer service issues. And in my experience, these two groups rarely overlap; your best customers will generate very few customer service problems.

Once you recognize these truths, you'll possess the key to rapid growth: bend over backwards for your best customers. These are the folks who'll spend the most money buying your products or services. They're the ones who'll help your small business thrive.

So, it's to your advantage to identify these exceptional customers. That way, you'll know where to spend the majority of your time and attention.

First, tally your sales revenue over the past 12 months.

Second, run a sales report that shows how much money each customer spent with you over this period.

Third, calculate the percentage of total sales revenue contributed by each customer. Do this by dividing each customer's sales volume by your total sales revenue, and multiplying the result by 100.

The above steps will reveal the top 20% of your customer base. These are the folks who deserve special attention. They're the ones for whom you should be willing to bend the rules.

Incidentally, you can (and should) take this concept one step further. We know 20% of your customers will generate 80% of your sales. We can also safely presume that 20% of *that* group - or 4% of your entire customer base - will generate 64% of your sales.

You don't need many of these "super" customers to run a commercially successful business.

Focus On Marketing Tactics That'll Have The Greatest Impact

Again, there are hundreds of ways to promote your small business. For example, you can attend trade shows, advertise on the radio, ask customers for referrals, write press releases, and hand out business cards to everyone you meet. Unfortunately, most of these practices will be a complete waste of time.

Above, we noted that the majority of your revenue will be generated by a small percentage of customers. In the same way, most of your sales will be generated by a small number of marketing tactics.

If you focus your time, effort, and capital on these ultra-effective tactics, you can produce staggering results in a relatively short time frame. In other words, use the 80/20 rule.

First, identify your target audience. Create a simple customer profile that defines your ideal customer. Include details such as age, gender, occupation, salary, and education.

Second, identify the best ways to reach this audience. You may find that your ideal customer discovers new products and develops brand loyalty via webinars. Or he or she might do so via social media, review websites (e.g. Consumer Reports), or simply by looking up specific terms on Google.

Third, identify the two most promising tactics. Devote the majority of your marketing resources to reaching customers through them.

It's tempting to try everything. But doing so will result in a lot of wasted time and money. Focus on the measures that work. You'll generate more revenue with less effort.

Find Your Most Profitable Products

Twenty percent of your products will generate 80% of your profit. It makes sense to focus your efforts on promoting the few products that generate the majority of your profit.

That's not to say you should ignore your low-margin products. After all, you might use some of them as top-of-the-funnel offers that encourage customers to buy more expensive products down the road. But it pays to discontinue low-margin offers that contribute little toward that end.

Doing so introduces two immediate advantages. First, it simplifies your product line. Greater simplicity leads to greater efficiency. Second, it gives you the freedom to focus your time on the few products that'll fuel your company's growth.

How do you identify your most profitable products? Follow these steps:

First, figure out the gross profit margin for each product in your line. Calculate gross profit by subtracting the cost of producing a product from the revenue generated by that product. Then, divide gross profit by the revenue figure, and multiply the result by 100.

Second, rank each product in your portfolio according to its gross profit margin.

Third, focus your marketing efforts on the top 20% of the products on this list. Also, consider discontinuing the bottom 20%, unless they're top-of-the-funnel offers.

Sales and marketing take a lot of time. The challenge is, time is arguably your most precious resource. Use the Pareto principle to streamline your marketing efforts, focusing your time where it'll have the biggest impact on your business.

BUILD AN ULTRA-PRODUCTIVE, HIGH-PERFORMANCE STAFF

~

I n terms of productivity, your employees are your greatest resource. But they can also represent one of your biggest time drains.

Consistent with the 80/20 rule, 20% of your employees will generate 80% of your business's productive output. They'll take on 80% of the responsibilities, come up with 80% of the solutions to existing challenges, and produce 80% of your leads and sales.

So it pays to identify your best employees, and give them the tools, autonomy, and guidance they need to do their jobs. The corollary is that you must also be able to identify your underperforming employees, and either coach them to improve their performance or let them go.

Developing a high-performance staff and keeping

them motivated will propel your business to new levels of sales and profitability. It begins with knowing who your hyper performers are and identifying their respective strengths.

Identify Your Employees' Talents

Each member of your staff will have strengths and weaknesses. Your job is to figure out how each member can best help your business to grow. The most effective way to do that is to utilize them in ways that leverage their talents.

For example, if your employee Tom is adept at sales, let him work his magic with customers and prospects. If your employee Sarah is a virtuoso at spreadsheets and possesses great analytical skills, let her handle the bookkeeping and financial reports.

It's not always easy to identify your employees' greatest strengths. But once you do so, you'll be able to let them loose in ways that'll have a massive impact on your company's success. Following are the simplest steps toward finding out how your employees can best help you.

First, ask them. Have a sincere conversation with each member of your staff. Encourage them to be specific about their skills. Just be aware they might express particular interests while being better suited for other duties.

Second, review your employees' employment histories. What did they do before you hired them? How long did they do it? Is there evidence of success - for example, multiple promotions?

Third, keep your eyes open. Observing your staff at work can be just as valuable as speaking to them. You'll invariably notice things certain employees do extremely well, from planning presentations and communicating with customers to analyzing data and solving tough problems.

Your employees' talents hold the key to improving your business's performance. The 80/20 rule advocates identifying and leveraging those talents.

Address Underperformance

One of the most difficult challenges for a business owner is knowing how to deal with underperforming employees. Once you identify underperformance, how do you manage it? How do you provide feedback without prompting an emotional confrontation? How do find out the reasons for the employee's lackluster performance so you can help them become more effective?

The Pareto principle suggests that 20% of your staff will generate 80% of your staff's performance-related problems. So it's worthwhile to address these problems head-on. Otherwise, you risk allowing them to fester and eventually bring down the morale of your entire team.

As you can imagine, some tactics are more effective than others. I recommend doing the following:

First, meet with the underperforming employee and highlight the performance issues that concern you. Be clear and direct about the changes you hope to see down the road.

Second, ask the employee why he or she thinks their performance has declined. You might gain a better understanding regarding what motivates him or her.

Third, discuss how you and the employee can work toward resolving the performance issues. Brainstorm solutions and schedule follow-up meetings to gauge the employee's progress.

This approach is more effective than aggressively reprimanding the employee and demanding improvements. It makes the employee feel valued, which will encourage him or her to perform better. There may be significant potential to cultivate and harness. With a bit of coaching, a problematic employee can become one of your star performers.

Outsource Low-Value Tasks

Operating capital is an ever-present constraint on small businesses. There's never enough money to do everything you want to do to grow your company. That includes hiring people.

It pays to maintain a lean staff. Let your trusted employees handle the most important tasks and activities, and outsource the rest. You'll keep your overhead at a manageable level, retain operational control, and benefit from the flexibility that comes with hiring talent (typically freelancers or independent contractors) on an as-needed basis.

If you're uncertain regarding what tasks to outsource and what tasks to keep in-house, do the following exercise.

First, make two lists. One list should include all tasks that are critical to your business strategy. The second list should include tasks that have little effect on your strategy.

Second, review the second list. Make a mark next to any tasks and activities that may become more important to your strategy in the future. For example, maintaining a blog may be unimportant at the moment. But it may become a core part of your marketing strategy at some point down the road. If so, hold off on outsourcing it.

Third, be willing to outsource every other task that appears on the second list. These low-value tasks are unlikely to require your expertise or that of your employees. Outsourcing them gives you and your staff the freedom to devote your specialized skills where they can produce the biggest results.

GROW YOUR BUSINESS WITH THE PARETO PRINCIPLE

~

We've seen in the previous sections the power of focusing on inputs that promise the best results in terms of growing your business. Specifically, we've talked about optimizing your sales and marketing efforts, streamlining your product line, and building a lean, hyper-productive staff.

In this section, we're going to build on those ideas.

You'll face daily decisions regarding new ways to expand your company's reach and generate more revenue. Some options will be winners and many will be losers. I'll demonstrate that, in accordance with the 80/20 rule, you and your business will be best served by focusing on the few things you know will work, and ignoring the rest.

Realize That Most Opportunities Are Distractions

Your business is in constant flux. It either grows or contracts. It never stays at the same level for long.

Assuming you're motivated to grow your company's revenues, you'll undoubtedly encounter an endless string of "opportunities." While the majority might sound promising, they're distractions. They'll spread you too thin and divert your attention to things that lie beyond your core competencies. Worse, they can become costly mistakes that threaten the long-term viability of your company.

Whenever you're presented with a new "opportunity," evaluate it according to the 80/20 rule.

First, ask yourself whether the opportunity aligns with your current business. If it doesn't, disregard it.

Second, consider whether your most valuable customers (your top 20%) have expressed a desire to purchase products or services related to the opportunity. If not, disregard it.

Third, think about whether the opportunity requires skills that you and your team lack. If it does, disregard it.

Diversification can be a great way to spur growth. But it's important to diversify in ways that allow you to leverage your current assets and resources. Any opportunity that doesn't allow you to do so is a distraction, and possibly a costly one.

Nurture And Coach Your Top-Performing Employees

We've discussed the value of building a high-performance staff. Having the right people in your company can lead to explosive growth. But hiring the right people is just the beginning. You must treat them in a way that keeps them motivated, improves their morale, and helps them to achieve their personal goals.

That's a tall order, especially when you're dealing with superstars.

The upside is that these high-value employees will be fiercely loyal to you and go to great lengths to perform well. If you treat them well, most will feel a sense of ownership in ensuring your business continues to be a success.

Nurturing top talent isn't a simple task. But if you give them the tools and offer the right blend of motivation and guidance, you'll see these employees flourish.

First, ask each of your high performers how you can support them in their jobs. Some of them will have specific ideas, such as making certain types of training available.

Second, implement a reward system for hitting goals. The rewards can take the form of monetary compensation. But realize that some employees prefer non-monetary rewards, such as paid vacation days. Sit down with each of your top performers and involve them in selecting their preferred rewards.

Third, challenge them. As good as your top performers are, they probably haven't reached their potential. Brainstorm ways to push them so they'll feel like they're experiencing professional (and even personal) growth.

It's crucial that you keep your top talent motivated and engaged. These employees represent your biggest levers in growing your company.

Seek New Customers That Fit Your Ideal Profile

Earlier, we discussed how 20% of your customers will generate 80% of your sales. Treat these high-value customers like gold. They're the cornerstone of your company's success.

Having said that, it's also important to have a steady stream of *new* customers enter your orbit. It's difficult to grow without constantly adding people to your customer base.

The key is to seek the *right* customers. They should fit your ideal customer profile, which will increase the likelihood they'll eventually graduate into your top 20%.

Not sure how to attract these valuable prospects? Try the following steps:

First, your ideal customer profile already includes details like age, gender, occupation, salary, and education. You should also have an idea regarding how to reach folks who fit this profile. Keep these details handy.

Second, create a marketing program designed to tap into one of these venues. For example, suppose your ideal customer discovers products and develops brand loyalty on social media. That being the case, create a marketing campaign to give your brand visibility and stimulate interest in your products on Facebook. Focus on one venue at a time. Otherwise, you risk spreading yourself and your resources too thin.

Third, brainstorm incentives that'll draw your ideal customer to you. This could be a hefty discount on your hottest-selling product. Or it might be a free gift delivered with the customer's first purchase. Depending on your business, you might offer free shipping, free financing, or free software that's relevant to your product line.

Running a small business isn't easy, especially when you have limited time and capital at your disposal. But you can use the Pareto principle to exert leverage in ways that can lead to tremendous, fast growth. It's as simple as focusing on the few inputs that generate the biggest outputs.

FINAL THOUGHTS ON 80/20 YOUR LIFE!

∽

8 0/20 *Your Life!* isn't about improving your career, your home life, relationships, diet and fitness routine, finances, training, or small business. It's about changing how you perceive the connection between your time and effort and the results you produce in every aspect of your life.

In short, this book is about adopting a new mindset. It's about recognizing that we can do more with less action. Best of all, we can apply that simple concept to every circumstance of our daily experience.

This single truth was an epiphany for me years ago. And I hope it is for you, too.

The 80/20 rule isn't a fancy concoction of the self-help industry. It's a law of nature that was present long before

Vilfredo Pareto noted its veracity in the late 1800s. It can be applied to everything around us.

The upside is that we can use this far-reaching principle to immediately change our lives for the better. All we have to do is acknowledge its truth and be willing to devote the majority of our attentional resources to the stuff that truly matters.

To be sure, this is a contrarian approach to life. Most people cling to a conventional perspective regarding inputs and outputs. They choose to believe these two facets are equally correlated. For example, you've undoubtedly heard people say, *"Just work hard and you'll succeed"* or *"If at first you don't succeed, try, try again."*

You know better. Success isn't just a matter of working hard or trying again. It's a matter of using leverage. That's the centerpiece of the 80/20 rule.

Over the next few weeks, I encourage you to look for evidence of the 80/20 rule in your life. Look for it everywhere. I have no doubt you'll quickly see how you can use it to get more done in less time, make faster decisions, and experience more confidence and happiness in the process!

DID YOU ENJOY READING 80/20 YOUR LIFE?

~

Thank you so much for reading *80/20 Your Life!* There's no shortage of personal development books out there, so I'm grateful that you've chosen to read mine. That means a lot to me.

May I ask you a small favor? If you got anything of value from *80/20 Your Life!*, would you take a moment and leave a review for the book at Amazon? A few words detailing what you enjoyed would be extremely helpful to me. It'll also inspire others to read the book.

One last note before we part ways...

I'll be writing additional books over the next several months. I plan to release each one at a steep discount. If you'd like to be notified when these books are released, and take advantage of the discounts, be sure to join my mailing list. As a bonus, you'll receive immediate access to my 40-page PDF ebook titled *Catapult Your Productivity! The Top 10 Habits You Must Develop To Get More Things Done.*

Join my list at the following address:

http://artofproductivity.com/free-gift/

I'll also send you my best productivity and time management tips via my email newsletter. You'll receive actionable advice on how to beat procrastination, create morning routines, avoid burnout, develop razor-sharp focus, and more!

If you have questions or would like to share a productivity tip that has made a measurable difference in your life, please feel free to reach out to me at damon@artofproductivity.com. I'd love to hear about it!

ALL THE BEST,

Damon Zahariades
http://artofproductivity.com

OTHER BOOKS BY DAMON ZAHARIADES

(AVAILABLE IN EBOOK, PAPERBACK, AND AUDIOBOOK
FORMATS)

~

The Joy Of Imperfection

Is perfectionism causing you to feel stressed, irritated, and
chronically unhappy? Here's how to silence your inner critic,
embrace imperfection, and live without fear!

The Art Of Saying NO

Are you fed up with people taking you for granted? Learn how
to set boundaries, stand your ground, and inspire others' respect
in the process!

The Procrastination Cure

Do you struggle with procrastination? Discover how to take
quick action, make fast decisions, and finally overcome your
inner procrastinator!

Morning Makeover

Would you like to start each day on the right foot? Here's how to
create quality morning routines that set you up for more daily
success!

Fast Focus

Are you constantly distracted? Does your mind wander after just a few minutes? Learn how to develop laser-sharp focus!

Small Habits Revolution

Got 5 minutes a day? Use this simple, effective plan for creating any new habit you desire!

To-Do List Formula

Finally! A step-by-step system for creating to-do lists that'll actually help you to get things done!

The 30-Day Productivity Plan

Need a daily action plan to boost your productivity? This 30-day guide is the solution to your time management woes!

The Time Chunking Method

It's one of the most popular time management strategies used today. Double your productivity with this easy 10-step system.

Digital Detox

Are you addicted to Facebook and Instagram? Are you obsessed with your phone? Use this simple, step-by-step plan to take a technology vacation!

For a complete list, please visit

http://artofproductivity.com/my-books/

ABOUT THE AUTHOR

~

Damon Zahariades is a corporate refugee who endured years of unnecessary meetings, drive-by chats with coworkers, and a distraction-laden work environment before striking out on his own. Today, in addition to being the author of a growing catalog of time management and productivity books, he's the showrunner for the productivity blog ArtofProductivity.com.

In his spare time, he shows off his copywriting chops by powering the content marketing campaigns used by today's growing businesses to attract customers.

Damon lives in Southern California with his beautiful, supportive wife and their frisky dog. He's currently staring down the barrel of his 50th birthday.

www.artofproductivity.com

Made in the USA
Monee, IL
17 February 2020